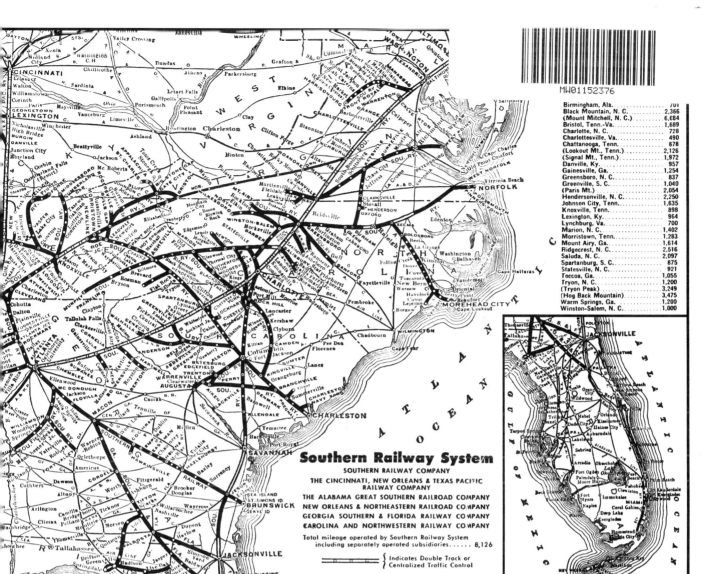

MW01152376

Birmingham, Ala.	701
Black Mountain, N. C.	2,366
(Mount Mitchell, N. C.)	6,684
Bristol, Tenn.-Va.	1,689
Charlotte, N. C.	728
Charlottesville, Va.	490
Chattanooga, Tenn.	678
(Lookout Mt., Tenn.)	2,126
(Signal Mt., Tenn.)	1,972
Danville, Ky.	957
Gainesville, Ga.	1,254
Greensboro, N. C.	837
Greenville, S. C.	1,040
(Paris Mt.)	2,054
Hendersonville, N. C.	2,250
Johnson City, Tenn.	1,635
Knoxville, Tenn.	898
Lexington, Ky.	964
Lynchburg, Va.	700
Marion, N. C.	1,402
Morristown, Tenn.	1,283
Mount Airy, Ga.	1,614
Ridgecrest, N. C.	2,516
Saluda, N. C.	2,097
Spartanburg, S. C.	875
Statesville, N. C.	921
Toccoa, Ga.	1,055
Tryon, N. C.	1,200
(Tryon Peak)	3,249
(Hog Back Mountain)	3,475
Warm Springs, Ga.	1,200
Winston-Salem, N. C.	1,000

Southern Railway System

SOUTHERN RAILWAY COMPANY

THE CINCINNATI, NEW ORLEANS & TEXAS PACIFIC RAILWAY COMPANY

THE ALABAMA GREAT SOUTHERN RAILROAD COMPANY
NEW ORLEANS & NORTHEASTERN RAILROAD COMPANY
GEORGIA SOUTHERN & FLORIDA RAILWAY COMPANY
CAROLINA AND NORTHWESTERN RAILWAY COMPANY

Total mileage operated by Southern Railway System
including separately operated subsidiaries...... 8,126

⎰ Indicates Double Track or
⎱ Centralized Traffic Control

ONLY ONE COUPON required, reading Southern Railway System between all points on or via lines mentioned above.

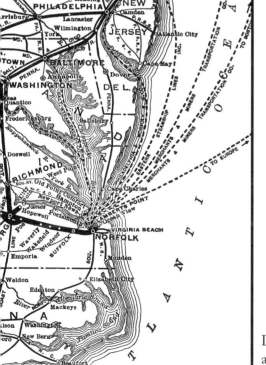

Left: The system map of the Norfolk and Western from 1944.

K. L. Miller Collection

Classic
STEAM TRAINS
OF THE SOUTH

BY

CURT TILLOTSON, JR.

Just down from mighty Saluda Grade, an Asheville, N. C. to Spartanburg, S. C. local freight is shown "resting" at the base of the grade, Melrose, N. C. in July of 1949, with 14 cars.

Frank Clodfelter/Collection of Tom Dixon

2000
TLC PUBLISHING INC.
1387 WINDING CREEK LANE
LYNCHBURG, VA 24503-3776

TABLE OF CONTENTS

COVER PHOTOS

The colorful Southern and Norfolk and Western are featured in this photo montage. The photos with detailed captions also appear in the color sections in this volume.

© Copyright 2000 TLC Publishing, Inc.

All rights reserved.
No part of this book may be reproduced without written permission from the publisher, except for brief excerpts used in reviews, etc.

Library of Congress Catalogue
Card Number 00-134726
ISBN 1-883089-55-7

Layout and Design by Kenneth L. Miller
Miller Design & Photography, Salem, Va.

Printed by
Walsworth Publishing Co. Marceline, Mo. 64658

Dedication

This book is lovingly dedicated to two individuals: one was my role model-the finest man I've ever known and respected; the other, an individual who loved me, cared for me, encouraged me and one who had all my love and affection. These two kind and gentle people were my dad and mom: Mr. Curtis C. Tillotson and Mrs. Alfreda D. Tillotson-I miss them so much!

Frank Clodfelter/Collection of Tom Dixon

INTRODUCTION AND ACKNOWLEDGEMENTS

When one talks of the time in rail history that steam power ruled the rails of our nation—believe it or not, there are still many of us "old timers" who can recall those glorious days-some will immediately conjure up memories of Union Pacific's huge 4-8-8-4 "Big Boys" storming up Sherman Hill or Southern Pacific's orange colored, semi-streamlined 4-8-4's cruising down the coast line between San Francisco and Los Angeles. What about those Milwaukee Road's 4-4-2's and 4-6-4 "Racers" on the "Hiawathas" or those sleek New York Central 4-6-4 Hudsons prowling up and down the river from which they were named, pulling the "Great Steel Fleet" and who could ever forget the Pennsy's 4-6-2's taking on mighty Horse Shoe Curve with a vengeance of steam and steel?

Yes, we all have our favorite roads, motive power and locations which fire up and strengthen those memories that help us to maintain our love of trains even during these times when mass-produced SD-70's, CW40-9's and similar behemoths keep the ribbon rails of today's railroads shiny and hot, pulling a great deal more tonnage faster and with fewer engines, albeit in a more sterile fashion.

Even with all the technological innovations that have enabled today's roads to prosper, when the term, "steam power," is mentioned, it brings a smile to the faces of many railfans (and most rail employees, as well). For your truly, the word "steam," immediately brings to mind railroads of the south, between the late 1920's until the early '50's, for railroading south of the Potomac River was special, you might, justly so-in my opinion-even say unique.

While many railroads were experimenting with newer, more powerful and efficient locomotives during the late 1930's and '40's, most southern roads relied on the standard and proven motive power such as 2-8-0's, 2-8-2's,

It's very cold this particular morning in January of 1946 when this photo was made. Mainline passenger local No. 11 is shown departing Spencer, N. C. (the station is seen on the right, in the background) at approximately 11:00 a.m. with a Southern Railway System Ps-4 class 4-6-2 beauty, No. 1374, providing the power for No. 11, which was a mail, express, baggage and passenger-"stop at all stations"-local.

By 1946, EMD diesels had replaced these majestic "ladies" on the main varnish between Washington and Atlanta, trains such as the Crescent, the *Piedmont Limited*, the *Southerner*, the *Peach Queen* and others; however, the locals were still operated by steam power and would continue to do so as late as 1952 (the Southern was completely dieselized by June of 1953). No. 135 & 136 and No. 11 & 12 usually had one of these elegant "ladies" up front.

Concerning No. 1374: look at the shine on that bell, the two brass "candlesticks" that bracketed the headlight and that brilliant number board under the headlight with a red background for the gold-colored numbers. The green and gold colors were still clean and eye-appealing. This scene is really a tribute to the care, the pride and attention given the steam engines, like No. 1374, by the Southern maintenance and engine crews right up to the very end of the steam era. Indeed, looking at No. 1374's dramatic departure this January morning, one could not conceive of the possibility that this and similar scenes would soon disappear forever.

No. 1374 was among the 2nd batch of Ps-4's delivered to the Southern in 1924 from Schenectady. The first batch (No.1375-1386), built in 1923, were so successful that the Southern purchased a second group of 15 Ps-4's with the same "specs" as the 1923 group: 73" drivers, 200 lbs. of boiler pressure, 304,000 lbs. of engine weight and a tractive effort of 47,500 pounds. No. 1374 served the Southern for 28 years, leaving the property in November of 1952.

The Ps-4's not only looked good and performed beyond the Southern's expectations, they also had a remarkable sound about them as well. With the cylinder-cocks slightly open, the sanders on, No. 1374's "stack talk" was sharp, distinct and memorable. Throw in that low, melodious steamboat whistle and you have another reason to consider the Ps-4's one of a kind when speaking of the Pacific-type steam locomotive.

The Ps-4's made a lasting impression on those of us who saw them. Through photos plus No. 1401-the only surviving Ps-4 (which can be seen at the Smithsonian Institute in Washington, D. C.)-this lasting impression continues to captivate everyone who admires grace, beauty and power in a steam locomotive.

Ray Carneal/Author's Collection

4-6-2's, 4-8-2's and articulated "Hogs" to move both people and tonnage right up to the end of the steam era. Meticulous maintenance, love and pride in these locomotives by the men who cared and operated them made it possible for these "relics" to roll up million of miles. They got the job done, even during World War II when rail traffic was almost unimaginable.

Of course, some roads south of the Mason-Dixon Line had modern steam power such as the 4-8-4's, 2-8-4's, 2-6-6-6's and a few other designs. The prime example of this modern motive power was the Norfolk & Western which, arguably, took the development of the steam engine to its limits with their renowned "Big 3:" class Y6b 2-8-8-2's, A class 2-6-6-4's and class J 4-8-4's. What about the C&O's gigantic 2-10-4's and the even larger, indeed a match of UP's "Big Boys," 2-6-6-6 Alleghenies? Still, the vast majority of power that kept things going until the advent and eventual domination of the diesel were of the common variety.

Who could ever forget the sight and thrill of a Southern Railway System Ps-4, green and gold colored, Elesco feedwater heater equipped, 4-6-2 coming out of one of the many dips on the busy Washington-Atlanta main line at 80+ m.p.h. and then start up the ensuing grade, wide-open, with staccato stack talk; a beautiful plume of smoke

shooting slightly above the engine before curving down and trailing off over the cars? With that melodious steam boat whistle tied down, it passed by you, bringing "goose-bumps" to your arms. You catch a brief glimpse of the engineer, with goggles on, looking ahead while "in his office" as a blur of white-rimmed wheels and flashing rods go by a most startled, wide-eyed young man who, with the ground trembling beneath his feet, forgot to count the cars since his eyes were glued on that magnificent piece of machinery upfront, still "shotgunning" and gathering momentum with every turn of its exceptionally clean wheels. Has man ever created a more "human-like" device than a steam locomotive going all-out and letting you know just what it was doing just by its sounds and actions?

What about a Seaboard Airline fruit extra heading north at a mile-a-minute to Richmond, Va. pulled by double-headed Q3 class 2-8-2's?

The RF&P and ACL 4-8-4's also made a lasting impression on those railfans standing trackside as they rolled by moving both passengers and mile long freights with great dispatch. The bullet nose N&W streamlined 4-8-4's created the same wonderful and unforgettable image.

One who watched a Southern Railway System 2-8-8-2 fighting for every inch of momentum up heavily sanded rails of Saluda

The J's pulled the best of the Norfolk and Western: the *Powhatan Arrow* (No. 25 and No. 26), the *Cavalier* (No. 15 and 16) and the *Pocahontas* (No. 3 and 4) plus some of the top varnish of the Southern Railway System (between Lynchburg, Va. and Bristol, Va.): the *Tennessean* (No. 45 and 46), the *Pelican* (No. 41 and 42) and the *Birmingham Special* (No. 17 and 18). The 600's also powered some local passenger trains as well, such as No.603- shown here passing through Bluestone, West Virginia and over the Bluestone River with 6 cars of No. 24 on June 15, 1950 (the Pocahontas Branch is seen on the left of the mainline).

Richard Cook/Author's Collection

Grade with a sound similar to cannons firing or a Clinchfield 4-6-6-4 taking on the Blue Ridge Mountains and not be moved by such a spectacle, would be one whose soul was dead-beyond recovery!

Even the southern short lines had a "magic" of their own. For example: how could one forget the sight of two Durham & Southern trim decapods blasting out of Durham, N. C. heading south to Apex and Dunn, N. C. or the Winston-Salem Southbound's ponderous ex-N&W 2-6-6-2's leaving the "Twin City, " i.e., Winston-Salem, N. C. for a journey to Wadesboro, N. C. with the grunting and groaning that only an old class Z could make?

Southern railroading was truly different from all other sections of our country. The engines and trains were aesthetically pleasing; the southern railroaders had a deep affection and pride for their locomotives, giving them a great deal of "TLC." This extra care enabled the older power to continue in operation for such a long period of time. They handled everything they were assigned on the main lines and branches in style until the diesel finally put them out to pasture. They might have been removed from the rails by the internal combustion power but they will always remain among our fondest memories. The younger railfans of today got an example of the charisma of the steam locomotive with the many and popular excursions in the 1970's and '80's, especially those operated by the Southern Railway System and later the Norfolk Southern Corp. (a road created by the merger of the Southern and the N&W in 1982).

This love, this appeal, this special enjoyment of the southern steam locomotive and its trains brings us to the purpose for this book. It is an attempt to preserve through photographs those days when steam operations were a common sight, for it was the only way railroads had of moving our country's business during those times.

Hopefully, through the following pages, those of us who grew up during this glorious era, will have our memories re-enforced. For the younger fans, it will provide a visual example of a time, now long gone, when every train-and I mean every train- was moved by steam, day and night, week after week, year after year.

At the outset, let me alert the reader that this effort is not an exhaustive historical look at the roads covered nor is it a book consisting of roster shots or a great deal of numbing statistical details. In fact, you will not find formal text, per say. What you might consider "text" will be found in the captions of each photograph. Instead, this book is designed to allow the reader to turn each page and slowly permit each scene depicted to be absorbed into one's memory, to simply enjoy each photo. It is an effort to bring a great deal of pleasure to the steam locomotive admirer.

Since many of the pictures found within the following pages were made by Ray Carneal-a long time Southern Railway System employee and resident of Durham, N. C.-a special section of the book will be devoted to steam railroading in and around his hometown, the "Bull City"-the nickname of this progressive Southern city; also his, and my beloved Southern will occupy over 50% of the photos in this endeavor to preserve an era now cataloged in the files called "Rail History."

This book would not have been possible without the dedication of those photographers who recorded on film those wonderful moments while most of us just watched the action unfolding before the young railfans. Such gentlemen include: Ray Carneal, Dave Driscoll, John Krause Tom Acree, Wiley Bryant, Frank Clodfelter, Richard Cook (all now deceased), Frank Ardrey, August Thieme Bob Malinoski and others.

A BIG "Thank You" goes to those railfans who contributed photos from their personal collections to help reinforce the effectiveness of this work. They include: Tom Dixon and Bill Griffin.

All who helped to make this book a reality have not only my deep appreciation but the admiration of those fans who are much better off because of this effort to preserve those times for others to both see and enjoy.

Curt Tillotson, Jr.
July 15, 2000

SOUTHERN RAILWAY SYSTEM

Passenger Power

What a pleasant and serene sight: a Southern Railway System Ps-4 class 4-6-2 (No. 1390) sitting at Raleigh's (N. C.) Union Station on a sunny, mild afternoon (6:00 p.m.) on May 3, 1949, with No. 13-a Goldsboro to Greensboro, N. C. local- and 5 cars.

The three lines serving Raleigh at this time: The Southern, Seaboard and Norfolk Southern, had used this old station for years; however, it was a stub end facility, requiring all trains to either back in or back out which was time consuming.

Who would think, on this day in 1949, that this grand scene would soon disappear: No. 1390, built by Schenectady in 1924 with 47,500 lbs.

of tractive effort, will be scrapped in 1953; No. 13 made its last run in 1964 (behind a diesel with 3 cars); the Southern will build its own station in 1950 near Cabarrus Street-now Raleigh's Amtrak Station-while SAL moved to their Johnson St. Yard area and built a fine depot in 1942 (The Eugene C. Bagwell Station); the old NS stopped using Union Station in 1940 (dropping all passenger service to the area in 1948) and Union Station will close and be removed shortly after this moment in rail history was preserved on film.

They say change is good. In this case, I'm not so sure if this is true.

Ray Carneal/Author's Collection

Coming at you is one of the most beautifully designed, most tastefully colored Pacific type of steam locomotive ever constructed. It had a distinctive symmetry which exuded the sense of poetry which made the Southern Railway System's green and gold painted Ps-4 class 4-6-2's a legend in their own time.

Even though all Ps-4's were exceptional in the "looks" department, most fans and other aficionados of the steam locomotive agree that the Ps-4's which were equipped with the Elesco feedwater heaters were a level above the other Southern 4-6-2's in regard to admiration, wonder and inspiration (your author is one who can be included in this group of admirers).

No. 6481, an Elesco feedwater heater equipped Ps-4 class 4-6-2, is shown working up Erlanger Hill (notice how white the southbound track appears which was due to a great deal of sanding) just south of Ludlow, Kentucky on the mostly double-track mainline of the Southern's CNO&TP (Cincinnati, New Orleans & Texas Pacific) with No. 3, the *Royal Palm*.

Called by many the "Rat Hole Division," the CNO&TP, at the time of this photo (summer of 1935), was dotted with tunnels, bridges, grades, sharp curves and close clearances. The tunnels were especially bad for the crews since many of the bores were located on grades; the blasting of the engine stacks caused material on the roof of the tunnels to break off and the smoke gave the engine crews a serious problem. To combat these conditions, a Southern engineer, B. A. Wimble, invented what became known as the Wimble Duct smoke deflector. When

entering a tunnel, the engineer could activate the device which was placed above the engine's sand and steam domes. It would move forward, cover the stack area and channel the smoke away from the cab. Passenger engines such as No. 6481 had short Wimble Ducts since passenger trains moved faster through the tunnels; freight engines had the longer version of the smoke deflector.

The *Royal Palm* ran from Chicago to Miami with the help of the New York Central, Southern and Florida East Coast; for many years it was the way for winter-weary tourists to head south for friendlier weather.

No. 6481, colored green and gold with white trimming and a remarkably clean graphite-covered smoke box, was built by Richmond in 1926, had 73" drivers, cylinders that were 27" x 28", a boiler pressure of 200 pounds and with an engine weight of 304,000 lbs., it could produce an impressive 47,500 lbs. of tractive effort. She served the Southern for nearly 27 years, being scrapped in May of 1953.

This photo is a prime example of the expression: "One picture is worth a thousand words." Add in the sounds of No. 6481's "stack talk" and the huge steamboat whistle plus the passage of the 10 passenger cars and you have a good "feel" of what it was like being at trackside during those wonderful days when steam ruled the rails.

Tom Acree/Author's Collection

By 1951, when this photo was made, it was unusual to find steam power in action on the Southern Railway System's Washington-Atlanta mainline. E-unit diesels had been assigned the name trains such as the *Crescent, Southerner, Tennessean* and others while the F-units had command of the hotshot freights. Steam was used as backup power for both the varnish and tonnage trains plus local freights and work trains.

Passenger locals such as No. 135 and 136 and No. 11 and 12, however, still used steam for power; usually the famous and still beautiful Ps-4 class 4-6-2's were assigned to these "stop at all station" runs and spent their remaining years in this type of service, like a champion boxer who continued to fight after his prime years.

This particular day in March of 1951, the boys in Spencer, N. C. did not have a Ps-4 available for No. 136, shown departing Lynchburg, Virginia's classic Kemper Street Station. As a result, they placed a big, fat, powerful Ms-4 class 2-8-2 to pull No. 136 to Monroe, Va. where a Ps-4 would carry the local on to Washington, D. C.'s Union Station.

Next to the Ps-4's the Ms-4 Mikados were among the most popular locomotive class with those who admired Southern's motive power.

No. 4814 came from the Richmond Works in 1923. It had 63" drivers, 200 lbs. of steam pressure along with an engine weight of 326,000 lbs. The heavy 2-8-2 mustered an impressive 59,600 lbs. of tractive effort; its tender held 16 tons of coal and 10,000 gallons of water and both engine and tender stretched to a length of approximately 83 feet. That huge Worthington feedwater heater was quite noticeable above No.4814's 3rd and 4th drivers and the reliable Hodge trailing truck was found on all 167 Ms-4's. Unfortunately, No. 4814 was retired in August of 1953.

For almost 30 years, the Ms-4 was the standard mainline freight locomotive on the Southern. The diesels eventually shoved them aside to lower assignments and, inevitably, to the scrapper's torch.

Even though the Elesco feedwater heater equipped Ms-4's were the most popular among the breed, old No. 4814 still looked good leaving Kemper Street and, if you closed your eyes and listened to its steamboat whistle and stack talk, you would swear it was a Ps-4.

I wonder what the crew thought back in Salisbury, N. C. when they discovered that their engine would be an Ms-4 freight "hog" rather than the usual, sleek Ps-4 for No. 136? Oh well, at least the dependable Standard style stoker was working.

Ray Carneal/Author's Collection

Queen In Her Court! Amid the smoke, cinders, grease and grime found at most engine terminals during the steam age, such as the Ivy City Facility (shown here) just north of Washington, D. C.'s Union Station, we find a "jewel." Not only was it a renowned, colorful Southern Railway System Ps-4 class 4-6-2, it was the one and only streamlined Ps-4, No. 1380.

Just off a run from Monroe, Va. (165 miles to the south), No. 1380 waits for the roundhouse crew who would refuel, water and wash this beauty in preparation for a return trip south on Southern's Washington Division this March day in 1942.

Many railroads got the "streamline craze" in the 1930's. By the end of this decade the Southern had made the decision to completely dieselize its entire motive power fleet. The needs of World War II were the major reasons why steam remained on the road that "Served the South" for so long (until July of 1953). In 1941, the Southern decided to re-equip its *Memphis Special* and rename it the *Tennessean* (Nos. 45 & 46). Along with a new train, the Southern also decided to have an engine streamlined to haul its new varnish.

The *Tennessean* would travel from Washington to Monroe where the Norfolk and Western would haul the train from Monroe to Bristol, Tennessee where it would be returned to the Southern for the final journey to Memphis, Tennessee. The N&W would not permit diesels on its property. As a result, the Southern decided to use steam for power on the Washington Division run since it did not want to tie down a few of its expensive diesels for such a short run.

Otto Kuhler, the respected industrial designer and mechanical engineer, created the design for this special locomotive and the Spencer (N. C.) shop crews put it all together. Why No. 1380? For one reason it was there (Spencer), it needed shopping and it did not have that famous Elesco feedwater heater.

What came out of Spencer shops in 1941 was, arguably, the most tasteful, colorful, aesthetically pleasing of all the streamlined steam locomotives ever built. The running board, which bore the name of the train it was designed to pull, i.e., the *Tennessean*, swept down into the front of the cylinders; the Southern symbol on the cylinders was a touch of genius and all moving parts were available to the servicing crews; even the tender was a thing of beauty! Kuhler, who was never paid for his effort, always maintained that the No.1380 project was his greatest achievement-I can surely understand why he would say this! No. 1380, in green, gold and white colors, was a sight to behold whether it was at rest or in action.

After the Washington Division dieselized No.1380 went into pool service along with several other Ps-4's and could be found anywhere on the mainline from Atlanta to Monroe. It remained the "Queen of the First Ladies" until the Southern retired her on July 29, 1953.

No. 1380 was built at Schenectady in 1923 and had a tractive effort of 47,500 lbs.

This photo was truly a portrait of beauty!

Ray Carneal/Author's Collection

LEFT

This photo, made at Monroe, Va. in January of 1948, had it all: 2 Southern Railway System Ps-4 Pacifics-No. 1366 (Schenectady-1924) and No. 1395 (Richmond-1926), a streamlined Norfolk and Western K2-class 4-8-2 No. 124 and an F-7 A+B+B+A set of General Motors diesels led by F-7A No. 4238. Talk about action-WOW!

And then there was the name: MONROE! Just mention the name to a railfan-Southern or otherwise-and it would be immediately recognized as a "railroad town." The song, "The Wreck of Old 97," had a passage: "They gave him his orders in Monroe, Virginia...," helped to make this small Virginia community part of the lexicon of the railfan's world.

On the Southern, Monroe was second only to Spencer, N. C. in recognition. At Monroe, the Danville Division ended and the Washington Division began. There was a railroad YMCA located here where accommodations were available for those train crews, in between runs, whose homes were elsewhere. Today nothing remains: No yard, no engine facilities, no crew change point-nothing to remind one of the importance this location once commanded. Everything was transferred to Lynchburg, Virginia's Montview Yard (9.5 miles to the south). It's a ghost town and today's trains move through the area is if it never existed. Still, scenes such as the one depicted here remain fresh in the minds of those who remember the times at Monroe when you could always find rail action each day, each night, each season of the year. Back then there was never a "shut down" for a holiday. It was business as usual, 365 days of each year.

The two green and gold colored Ps-4's are shown being readied for another passenger assignment to Washington or Salisbury, N. C.; the N&W "streamliner" awaits another passenger run to Bristol, Tenn. via Roanoke with one of the three Southern varnishes that took this route: the *Tennessean,* the *Birmingham Special,* and the *Pelican,* and the four diesels will soon power one of the many through freights to Spencer and points south.

Dave Driscoll/Author's Collection

Even though this particular Southern Railway System's Ps-4 class 4-6-2, shown in the photo, carries the first number (No. 1366) in their classic Pacific series, it was actually NOT the first of the Ps-4 group of locomotives. The first Ps-4's received by the Southern came from Schenectady in 1923 (No. 1375-1386). Since these heavy, USRA designed 4-6-2's proved to be so successful, the road ordered a second batch from Schenectady which were delivered to the Southern in 1924. They were numbered No. 1366-1374 and No. 1387-1392.

Regardless of these facts, No. 1366 (even after 26 years of service) still cuts a most handsome figure in 1950, late in the steam era on the Southern which was completely dieselized by June of 1953. No. 1366 is pictured approaching Reidsville, N. C. on the double-track, automatic block protected mainline this sunny morning, June 5, 1950, with local No. 11, carrying 7 cars on its Monroe, Va. to Greenville, S. C. run. The green and gold-colors and white-trimmed wheels of No.1366 are still clean and eye appealing. Unfortunately, the big 4-6-2 only had 2 more years of service remaining before being replaced by diesels. Sadly, No. 1366 was removed from the roster on July 29, 1953.

Although by 1950 more and more diesels were keeping these rails shiny, whenever No. 11 and 12, as well as locals No. 135 and 136, appeared behind a Ps-4, with that big steamboat whistle announcing their arrival, one's memory of the glorious steam era was reinforced and we could revel in the sights and sounds of these beautiful locomotives which dominated the Southern's passenger fleet for so many wonderful years. How could any diesel duplicate such a scene of steam and steel in action?

Dave Driscoll/Author's Collection

The Southern Railway System was renowned for the care they lavished on its motive power. This photo of Ms-4 class 2-8-2 No. 4879 was a prime example of the pride Southern crews had for their locomotives.

I defy anyone to identify a more beautiful aesthetically pleasing freight locomotive on any railroad. No. 4879 was a freight engine. It was not prepared for an excursion or any special occasion. The heavy Mikado was simply pictured on the ready track at Asheville, N. C. in June of 1935 after receiving shopping from the Asheville maintenance crews.

Even though such "TLC" was given their engines all over the Southern, the Asheville Division "boys" seemed to have given an extra amount of "love" to the locomotives assigned to their division. Just look at No. 4879: white rimmed wheels, running board, cowcatcher and other parts, graphited smokebox, shiny black colored engine, yellow numbers and lettering; look at those cylinder heads and the super clean appearance over the entire engine. No. 4879's bell, in front of the Elesco feedwater heater, appeared to be brand new since it was so clean-straight from the factory. Those "safety first" signs on the cowcatcher were immaculate and a nice touch!

No. 4879 was built by Richmond in 1926 and was one of 167 Ms-4 class heavy "Mikes" to roam over the Southern for many years. It had 63" drivers, 200 lbs. of steam pressure plus an engine weight of 326,000 pounds. The tender, which weighed 191,360 lbs., carried 16 tons of coal plus 10,000 gallons of water; with a tractive effort of nearly 60,000 lbs. The Ms-4's were the standard mainline power on the Southern from 1923 until they were pushed aside by the diesels. Being 83 feet long, No. 4879 was finally retired in November of 1952.

Normally found on the Washington-Atlanta mainline and the CNO&TP, they could also be seen in other "big rail" areas as well. Occasionally, you would even find them on the Asheville Division territory-an area populated mainly by 2-10-2's, 2-8-8-2's, 4-8-2's plus lighter M-class Mikados and Consolidations.

Next to the colorful Ps-4's, the Ms-4's were among the most popular class of motive power on the Southern. Looking at this excellent photo, it is easy to understand the affection given these heavy 2-8-2's by those who admired the compact, good-looking and reliable locomotives of the Southern Railway System.

I can remember seeing the Ms-4's passing through Durham and Greensboro, N. C. as well as Greer, S. C. (my Dad's hometown). They certainly made a lasting impression on this young man!

Frank Clodfelter/Author's Collection

Look at the earthen left bank in this picture: totally covered with cinders, several inches deep. Now look at the bank on the right of the Southern Railway System's Washington-Atlanta mainline: No cinders of consequence!

The area shown is just north of Monroe, Va. at the beginning of the Washington Division. The cinders on the east side of the mainline resulted from the thousands of trains, over several decades of steam operations, leaving Monroe, blasting upgrade north towards Potomac Yard and Washington, D. C.'s Union Station. On the other hand, southbound trains at this location were coasting towards the crew change point stop and not spewing out cinders which resulted in a clean, west side embankment.

No. 136 was shown department Monroe in September of 1950 with Ps-4 class 4-6-2 No. 1408, pulling 11 cars of this mail, express and passenger local, heading north with the enthusiasm that only the green and gold colored class of heavy Pacifics could produce.

Not a diesel in sight! Indeed, if you did not know the date of this photograph, you might suspect it was sometimes between the late 1920's or the 1930's when steam was king and the Ps-4's were the queens of the Southern's passenger fleet.

No. 1408 was a product of Baldwin (1928) and among the last batch of Ps-4's to arrive on the property. The Elesco feedwater heater, mounted in front of its stack, simply added to the aesthetic appeal of this green and gold beauty. Add that deep and haunting steamboat whistle and you have a legend! No. 1408 was retired in October of 1952.

The staccato stack talk of No. 1408 sounded like a machine gun as No. 136 was already up to 40 m.p.h. and increasing in speed with every revolution of its white rimmed drivers.

To watch a Ps-4 pass by was like watching poetry in motion. It was a sight that stirred the soul and succored the love the railfans had for not only the magnificent Ps-4's but other steam power as well. The right sights, sounds, smells and feel of the steam locomotive were combined into one when viewing a Ps-4 in action.

Ray Carneal/Author's Collection

When the Southern Railway System T-class 4-8-2's first arrived on the property in 1917, they were immediately assigned to mainline passenger service, including the Washington-Atlanta run. As more Ps-4 heavy Pacifics appeared, however, the Mountains were gradually replaced from mainline duties and transferred to the Asheville and other mountainous divisions. Eventually, they were concentrated in and around the Asheville, N. C. area, pulling passenger trains up and down Saluda Grade to and from Spartanburg, S. C. or Salisbury, N. C. and from Asheville to Knoxville and Chattanooga, Tennessee plus a few other areas where mountains had to be conquered.

By February of 1949, when this exposure was made, it was becoming unusual to still find the 4-8-2's on the Washington-Atlanta mainline. No. 1480, a Southern Ts-1 class Mountain-all green and gold in color-built by Baldwin in 1919, is shown pulling No. 135-10 cars of mail, express and one passenger coach on the rear-between Monroe and Lynchburg, Va. over the classic James River Bridge, approximately two miles north of Lynchburg's Kemper Street Station (its next stop).

This bridge was one of the marvels not only on the Southern but throughout the railroad world as well. It crosses over both the historic James River and the Chesapeake & Ohio's James River line-between Clifton Forge and Newport News, Va. (under the south end of the bridge).

Today only one track, the old southbound main, still spans the river and now the CSX. It is one of the short, single-track sections of the C. T. C., automatic block, microwave protected Washington-Atlanta mainline.

I have taken several photos of trains crossing this magnificent structure from the north end, including most of the steam power used in the excursion program, and I never cease to be amazed at the sight of a long freight or varnish making 40+ m.p.h. across the long bridge which would continue to "rumble" for nearly half-a minute after the train had passed. The James River Bridge still remains one of the "wonders of the rail world"-at least to me!

No. 1480 had 69" drivers, 200 lbs. of steam pressure, an engine weight of 327,000 pounds plus a tractive effort of 53,900 lbs. It was almost 87 feet long and 15 feet high, with a tender that carried 16 tons of coal and 10,000 gallons of water.

As a point of interest, No. 1480, which was retired in August of 1953, had its headlight on because it was approaching the Rivermont Park tunnel at the south end of the bridge-a tunnel which was daylighted many years ago.

Just look at those rails: shiny enough to see how to shave by. It was truly a wonderful sight to witness, one that would remain with you forever!

Both: Ray Carneal/T.W. Dixon Jr. Collection

What a great setting and the perfect way to start a railfanning day: the impressive George Washington National Masonic Memorial (on the left), a busy 4-track main line and an immaculate Southern Railway System Ps-4 class 4-6-2 opening up as it leaves the Alexandria, Va. area for a trip south over the rails of the RF&P. As I said: it's going to be a great day for a railfan with a camera.

Within a mile No. 1396, shown here in all its elegance, pulling No. 135 on the Washington Division this November 1949 morning at 8:25 a.m., will leave RF&P territory and enter Southern's historic Washington-Atlanta main line with gathering momentum.

The two tracks on the left were used for passenger trains while the two outside tracks hosted the many freights entering and leaving huge Potomac Yard. Trains of not only the Southern and RF&P passed through here but those of the C&O also helped to keep the 4 tracks shining and busy. Indeed, the traffic into and out of Alexandria was, and remains tremendous!

Shortly after arriving on Southern rails from the Richmond Locomotive Works in 1926, No. 1396 had a Crescent Moon painted in gold on the side of its cylinders and on its tender the name, "Crescent Limited" was also painted in gold. This Ps-4 powered the historic varnish, whose cars were colored to match the green and gold 4-6-2 upfront, for several years. No. 1396 was retired in February of 1952.

Even though No. 1396 was assigned to main line local No. 135 this brilliant morning, it still appears as beautiful as when she was at the headend of No. 37, the *Crescent Limited*. The Southern's maintenance crews made sure that these exceptionally beautiful "ladies" looked their very best until the bitter end. Fortunately, with photos such as this one, we can always remember them in action, continuing to work for the company and making a lasting and fond memory for all who saw them in regular service.

Both: Ray Carneal/T.W. Dixon Jr. Collection

It's approximately 3:30 p.m. this sunny afternoon in June of 1951 as we find the still elegant, green and gold colored Southern Railway System Ps-4 class 4-6-2 No. 1406 at the head of mainline "stop at all stations" mail, express and passenger local No. 136 in Monroe, Virginia ready for a leisurely run to Washington, D. C.

By 1951, steam had all but disappeared on the Southern since the diesels-some say the "savior" while others called them names I will not go into-had made tremendous inroads on the Southern's roster. A case in point was this scene, captured on film, of the past and future motive power working together. The famous Ps-4's, which used to power such historic varnish as the *Crescent, Piedmont Limited, Peach Queen* plus other similar passenger runs, had been relegated to such plug assignments as No. 135 and No. 136 and the lowly No. 11 & 12.

Next to one of these "First Ladies of the Pacifics" was an A+B+B+A set of GM's F-7 diesels, led by No. 4206 (all being readied for a through freight to Potomac Yard). No. 4206 and its mates were "youngsters" with at least 20 years of service in its future. No. 1406, however, was an "old-timer" (coming to the Southern from Baldwin in 1928) and would be retired in November of 1952-just slightly over a year of service remaining for this most attractive lady.

No. 1406 had 73" drivers, 200 lbs. of steam pressure plus an engine weight of 304,000 lbs.-all helping to produce 47,500 pounds of tractive effort.

Until the day these renowned 4-6-2's left the rails for good, they remained aesthetically pleasing to the eye, compact yet sleek and the Southern crews lavished much attention on their Ps-4's. These heavy Pacifics truly deserved the reputation for beauty and performance they created on the Southern between the late 1920's until 1953.

LEFT:

One in and one out. The rail traffic on the Southern Railway System in the Monroe, Va. area during the steam era was almost continuous. A case in point is shown in this photo, which was made just north of Monroe on January 27, 1950, with a snowbound freight in from Potomac Yard (shown on the right) as a magnificent, green and gold colored, Richmond built (1926) Ps-4 class Pacific roars by, heading north to Washington, D. C.'s Union Station with mainline local passenger, mail and express No. 136 in a grandeur that only a Ps-4 could create.

The "captain" (conductor), from the Washington Division, is shown getting back on his "crummy" (caboose) as a Danville Division crew starts the freight south towards Spencer, N. C. Once at the Monroe station, he will drop-off (on the fly) to be replaced by a Danville Division conductor. No. 136, coaled and watered at Monroe, also had a new crew on board that would carry the varnish all the way to our nation's capital.

No. 1397, had that beautiful and efficient Elesco feedwater heater in front of its stack Ps-4's No. 1393-1404 were equipped with 6-wheel tender trucks (the other heavy Pacifics had tenders with 4-wheel trucks). As a result, they carried 14,000 gallons of water plus 16 tons of coal. Eventually, their coal bunkers were built up and they could carry almost 20 tons of the black fuel.

Monroe used to be a favorite location for both train photographers and watchers, for you could get a least 3 pictures of the same train: coming into town, changing crews and then leaving the location; during steam operations this opportunity was truly appreciated.

Even though Monroe has now been downgraded to an almost "ghost town" status, you can still watch the mainliners pass by. For those of us old enough to remember when steam power was commonplace, we can still visualize Ps-4's in action or equally attractive Ms-4 "Mikes" at the head of through freights and Norfolk and Western J-class 4-8-4's or K2-class 4-8-2's-all streamlined-heading into or going south out of this once "hot" railroad town: Monroe!

Ray Carneal/T.W. Dixon Jr. Collection

On this cool November morning in 1935, Southern Railway System's passenger train No. 3, the *Royal Palm*, had 16 cars out of Cincinnati, Ohio. This was far too much tonnage for the road engine, Ps-4 class 4-6-2 No.6482, to climb Erlanger Hill, a few miles south of Cincinnati. As a result, a beefy Ms-1 class Mikado, No. 6292, was placed in front of the elegant Ps-4 to help her get No. 3 over the hill.

The *Royal Palm* was the Southern's premier train on the CNO&TP (Cincinnati, New Orleans & Texas Pacific) so it was assigned their best passenger power, the Ps-4 Pacifics, to help No. 3 complete its journey from Chicago to Miami, with the help of the New York Central (Chicago-Cincinnati) and the Florida East Coast (Jacksonville-Miami).

No. 6482 was a Richmond-built (1926) 4-6-2. The helper, No. 6292, was a 2-8-2 class Ms-1 built by Schenectady in 1918.

Once beyond Erlanger Hill (approximately 7-8 miles long-south of Ludlow, Kentucky) No. 6292 will be removed and Ps-4 No. 6482 will take the tourist heavy varnish south toward Chattanooga and beyond.

What a grand sight: a clean freight "hog" colored in black with yellow numbers and lettering plus a graphite-covered smokebox, helping a brilliantly green and gold sheathed, white trimmed wheels, classic Ps-4, both wide-opened on the double-track "Rat Hole Division," as many called the CNO&TP, heading No. 3 over this magnificent, heavy-duty bridge. Can you imagine the sounds that must be emanating from such an earth-shaking event?!

Due to the numerous tunnels that dotted the old "Rat Hole," No. 6482 had a Wimble Duct smoke deflector to help the crew survive the smoke and gasses that became a dangerous factor in those tunnels. The helper did not have a smoke deflector but it did have a small light placed before its stack, so, at night, the fireman could see how much smoke was coming out of his Mikado-less smoke meant a more efficient use of the company's coal.

It is with great thanks that there was a photographer on hand this particular day in November of 1935 to record this unforgettable scene on film so that future generations of railfans could see just how it was during that grand era when steam ruled the rails of the Southern.

Wouldn't it be wonderful if only we could time travel back to the 1930's so that we may watch such scenes once more?

Tom Acree/Author's Collection

By March 23, 1950, when this photo was made, steam-powered passenger trains were becoming a rare sight on the Southern. Such mainliners as *The Crescent, Southerner, Piedmont Limited* and others had diesels on the point. On locals, however, you could still find steam in command, prowling the rails they knew so well for so many years, years when they and not the diesels pulled the finest passenger trains offered by the Southern.

Here, in Salisbury, N. C. (at 1:25 p.m.), we find two majestic Ps-4 type 4-6-2's. No. 11, a "stop-at-all-stations" local, came in from Monroe, Va. behind No. 1383 (shown on the right). No. 1387 will continue No. 11's journey south within minutes while No. 1383 will head for the roundhouse in Spencer for servicing.

Even though they were assigned to such "plug" runs in these dying days of steam operations, both Ps-4's had their trademark, and most pleasing to the eye, green and gold color scheme. They were built by Schenectady-No. 1383 in 1923 and No. 1387 in 1924; both carried 200 lbs. of steam pressure, had 73" drivers and produced 47,500 lbs. of tractive effort.

Unfortunately, their days were numbered by 1950 as more and more diesels were added to the Southern's roster. Indeed, No. 1383 was retired in February of 1952 and No. 1387 left the property just two months later; however, this mild, clear March day, one can still remember how it used to be, when these grand ladies were the main power for the Southern's fleet of historic varnish.

They kept their dignity until the very end and they still warm the blood of their admirers whenever one mentions the Southern's great Ps-4 Pacifics.

Ray Carneal/Author's Collection

Coming in from Monroe, Va. passenger local No. 11 is shown arriving in Salisbury, N. C. headed by Southern's class Ps-4, 4-6-2, No. 1404 (built in 1926 by the Richmond Locomotive Works with 47,500 lbs. of tractive power and 73" drivers).

Waiting to replace No. 1404 is Ps-4 No. 1407 (seen on the left). No. 11 will continue its journey south on the Washington-Atlanta main line behind this "fresh" green and gold colored 4-6-2, built by Baldwin in 1928, making stops at nearly all stations along the way.

As more diesels appeared on the property, the once mighty Ps-4's were assigned to such unglamorous runs as No. 11 until all steam disappeared on the Southern in June of 1953 (No. 1404 and No. 1407 were "retired" in 1952).

Still, on this July 31, 1950 day, we can see the power, in action, that once hauled the historic varnish of the Southern such as the *Crescent Limited* at work on the main line at one of the most famous locations on the road that "Served the South"—the Spencer-Salisbury area.

Amtrak's *Carolinian, Piedmont* and *Crescent* still serve this location today; however, the old station is no longer in use. Amtrak built a much smaller facility at the south end of this once beautiful structure to handle their patrons.

Ray Carneal/Author's Collection

LEFT:

Southern's green and gold colored, white trimmed Ps-4, No. 1398, pulling passenger train No. 36, the *New Orleans-Atlanta-Washington Express*, nears Alexandria, Va., its last stop before reaching its destination: Washington, D. C.'s Union Station. The arrival and departure of these green and gold beauties were the most attractive and admired of all the steam engines passing through this very busy area each and every day.

No. 1398 was built by Richmond in 1926 and had an Elesco feedwater heater located between the smokestack and bell. Most steam connoisseurs, including yours truly, always felt that the Elesco feedwater heater equipped Southern Ps-4's were the most attractive, the most aesthetically pleasing of all the engines in this famous series of colorful steam power.

The boys in Monroe, Va. made sure this elegant lady had fresh graphite on its smoke box, white trimmed drivers and cylinder heads and the green and gold paint was clean even though by 1949 more and more diesels were replacing them as the main power on the Southern's famous fleet of varnish. No. 1398 will continue to serve the company until it was retired in January of 1952 after romping up and down the main line for almost 27 years.

No. 36 was a semi-main line local which left New Orleans the day before this photo was made in October of 1949 at approximately 5:15 p.m.

The two tracks on the right were used for passenger trains while the two tracks to the left of No. 1398 were prowled by the freights going into and out of Potomac Yard. All four heavy-duty tracks belonged to the Richmond, Fredericksburg and Potomac and the area was a railfan's delight for watching the tremendous volume of trains that graced these rails at this time, day and night. Oh to be that engineer in the cab of one of the railroad's most beautiful locomotives!

John Krause/Author's Collection

No. 1380 is shown in Reidsville, N. C. on March 29, 1952, at the head of the mainline passenger local No. 11.

As the Southern approached complete dieselization, No. 1380 and the other Ps-4's still in operation by 1952, were given such lowly runs as No. 11, which traveled from Monroe, Va. to Greenville, S. C., stopping at nearly every station along the way, carrying mostly mail, express and baggage plus one or two coaches.

No. 1380 was built by Schenectady in 1923. It kept its streamlining until she was retired on July 29, 1953.

Dave Driscoll/Author's Collection

Replacing a sister Ps-4 from Monroe, Va. (the steam from the safety valve of the other 4-6-2 can be seen above the 3rd car), main line local passenger No. 11, powered by No. 1387, is shown departing the station in Salisbury, N. C. this March 23rd day of 1950, heading south on the busy Washington-Atlanta main line of the Southern Railway System at 1:30 p.m. with a most dramatic flair!

The dying days of steam operations on the Southern found these elegant ladies that once powered the finest varnish in the South, demoted to such lowly assignments as this "stop-at-all stations" local.

Even though her time was nearly at an end, the Southern employees still kept these "Queen of the Pacifics," as one railfan aptly called the Ps-4's, looking beautiful. Look at the shine on No. 1387's tender along with the white striping.

Yes, this Schenectady built (1924) lady maintained her dignity right up to the very end which, for No. 1387, was April 1, 1952.

What a wonderful sight!

Ray Carneal/Author's Collection

LEFT:

When a passenger train arrived in Marion, N. C. on June 9, 1950, you could always find a good-size crowd at the station—a wonderful sight! There were passengers to get on, people to get off; express, mail and some L-C-L to transfer and there were many on hand just to see this daily drama unfold—train watchers. Yes, in 1950, people could still be found at the station when it was train time.

The center of attention this particular day is Southern Railway System's train No. 21, the *Carolina Special,* pulled by one of the Southern's long and lean, green and gold colored, white trimmed Ts-1 class 4-8-2, No. 1480, with 9 cars tied on behind its shiny tender.

This is the Goldsboro, N. C. section of the Cincinnati-Chicago bound varnish. In Asheville, N. C. No. 21 will be combined with the section from Charleston, S. C. (No. 27). As one train the *Special,* No. 27, will head for Cincinnati, Ohio and then, over the rails of the New York Central, complete its journey to Chicago, Illinois.

Mountain type 4-8-2's powered all passenger trains west of Salisbury, N. C. in order to cope with the Blue Ridge Mountains which abruptly rose up just west of Marion.

No. 1480, an Asheville Division assigned Ts-1, was built by the Baldwin Locomotive Works in 1919 and produced 53,900 lbs. of tractive effort on 69" drivers with 200 pounds of stream pressure and had an engine weight of 327,000 lbs. Due to the numerous sharp curves in the mountains, the Ts-1's were equipped with "floating" front drivers to help them better negotiate the curves.

No. 1480 was retired in June of 1953 after spending 34 years of battling and conquering the curves, grades, tunnel and hard weather encountered in the Blue Ridge Mountains.

The Asheville Division crews kept these beloved giants clean and beautiful right up to the end of their rein in the mountains. They were truly "Ladies of the Mountains" and served the Southern and the citizens of the South with distinction and grace until replaced by the diesels.

It is a cold February 22, 1947 afternoon and some snow can still be found, even two days after a winter storm passed through the area—all ingredients necessary to product this superb photo which was taken at 3:30 p.m.

Train No. 21, the *Carolina Special,*—a name steeped in rail history—is shown leaving Marion, N. C. in a symphony of sights and sounds with Ts-1 class 4-8-2 No. 1487 at the head of the 9 cars on this Cincinnati and Chicago bound Southern Railway System passenger train.

No. 1487 was built by Baldwin in 1919 and was finally retired from service in November of 1952.

All: Ray Carneal/Author's Collection

Crossing over the Atlantic Coast Line's double track mainline in Selma, N. C. is Southern Railway System's local passenger train No. 14 from Greensboro, N. C. on May 16, 1949 at 10:25 a.m., headed by Ps-4 class 4-6-2 No. 1391.

With only one more stop to make before reaching its destination, Goldsboro, N. C., No. 1391, with 5 cars, leaves the station, which serves both the Southern and ACL, in a potpourri of smoke and sounds—a sight that one who was there could never forget.

By 5:05 p.m. this same day, No. 1391 will pass through Selma once more, this time pulling local No. 13 westbound back to Greensboro.

At this time the Southern provided Selma with 6 passenger trains (3 east, 3 west) with the *Carolina Special* being THE mainliner—all pulled by the majestic and captivating Ps-4. No. 1391 was a prime example of this breed of locomotive which, to this very day, has a reputation of beauty, perfect symmetry and beloved by all who saw them throughout the late 1920's into the early 1950's when steam left the Southern for good.

No. 1391 was born at Schenectady in 1924. It was finally removed from Southern rails in November of 1952.

Even after 25 years of service and probably a million miles or more of travel, No. 1391 still looks grand in her renowned green and gold colors with white trim, even now when it had been bumped from the mainline by the ever increasing number of diesels, and assigned to such locals as No. 14. The appearance of No. 1391 is a tribute to the Southern crews who cared for them all those years giving the extra attention, love and respect they justly deserved. This affection bestowed upon these great ladies can explain, to a large degree, why they remained not only in service for such a long period of time but so eye pleasing as well.

This extra north originated in Spencer Yard (N. C.) earlier in the day to help make room for more cars at this historic facility, in November of 1949. Now the big Southern Ms-4, 2-8-2, is shown nearing Alexandria, Va., and its destination: the huge and busy Potomac Yard; No. 4814 is now on the rails of the Richmond, Fredericksburg and Potomac Railroad.

Even though No. 4814 has only 4 more years to serve the Southern (built at Richmond in 1923) No. 4814 still appears clean and ready to haul more tonnage for another 30 years. Unfortunately, like many of its sister Ms-4, the big "hog" will be retired in 1953.

She has 27" x 32" cylinders, an engine weight of 326,000 lbs. and carried a Worthington feedwater heater on 63" drivers.

This area was, and remains, and excellent "train-watching" location, for traffic through here is tremendous!

John Krause/Author's Collection

Passing under Boylan Street overpass and leaving the jointly operated (Southern-Seaboard) double track section of tracks which extends from Cary to Raleigh's Boylan Tower (to the left of the overpass from which this photograph was made), Southern's through freight No. 254, from Greensboro and Spencer, N. C., is seen entering Raleigh, N. C. on its journey to Selma, N. C. Ms-4, No. 4834, a Richmond built (1923) 2-8-2 with 59,600 lbs. of tractive effort and 63" drivers, has 58 cars this May 3, 1949 at 3:10 p.m.

The Seaboard's main line to Richmond, Va. is seen above the "reefer" behind No. 4834's shiny tender angling off to the left while Raleigh's old Union Station can also be seen above the same "reefer."

The Engineer of No. 4834, which will be retired in April of 1952, looks ahead as No. 254 prepared to cross over busy Cabarrus Street on its eastbound trek.

It will be mostly all down grade to Selma as No. 254 leaves the rolling terrain of the Piedmont section of North Carolina and enters the Coastal Plains which leads down to the Atlantic Ocean. The big Ms-4 will not have any problems getting its tonnage to Selma and a connection with the Atlantic Coast line.

This location remains one of the best places for train-watching in Raleigh to this very day.

Ray Carneal/Author's Collection

Southern Railway System

Freight Power

Acres and acres of Pacifics, Consolidations, Santa Fes, Mikados and even a few GM F-7 diesels: all a railfan could wish for are found in this "busy" photograph made at the historic Spencer (N. C.) Shops in June of 1948.

Since Spencer was not only mid-point on the Southern Railway System's hot Washington-Atlanta mainline but the end of their strategic line from Asheville, N. C. as well, the Southern decided to build its shop facilities here plus a large freight yard which included an area to ice down an entire refrigerator train loaded with sweet-tasting peaches and other perishable items.

By World War II, nearly 2,500 men were employed by the Southern in the Spencer area which also included a large, attractive railroad YMCA that was always busy since 3 divisions converged on this small North Carolina town, just north of much larger Salisbury: Danville (from Monroe, Va. and Selma, N. C.), Charlotte (from Greenville, S. C.) and Asheville (from the "Land of the Sky").

With the arrival of heavier, longer and more powerful engines in the 1920's, the Southern "modernized" and enlarged all facilities in Spencer: a 37-stall roundhouse, several offices, a larger yard and a shop area that could put together a locomotive from the wheels up.

Just look at the motive power collected here this June day in 1948:

(r-to-l) Ps-4 class 4-6-2 No. 1390, Ks class 2-8-0 No. 728, Ps-4 No. 1408 and 2 other sisters, a huge Santa Fe 2-10-2, a group of Ms-4 class 2-8-2's and two sets of GM's highly impressive and successful F-7 diesels — WOW!

By 1953, all steam locomotives were gone from Southern rails and the employment at Spencer had dropped off dramatically; many of the facilities shown here were gone. It appeared that only the yard would remain since diesels could travel the entire length of the Washington-Atlanta main.

Fortunately, in the mid-1970's a group of North Carolinians began work to preserve Spencer Shops. By 1979, Southern president L. Stanley Crane had contributed 57 acres of land plus 13 shop buildings to the preservation group. In September of 1977, North Carolina's Governor Jim Hunt accepted the deed to the first area of land given to the state by President Crane in front of the Master Mechanic's office. Thus was born the North Carolina Transportation Museum that can be visited to this very day with steam and diesel engines, rolling stock plus other transportation items on display.

Oh, for the opportunity to walk among so much steam and diesel power once again when the name "Spencer Shops" meant big-time railroading in action.

Originally an 0-6-0 switcher which was built by Baldwin in 1906, this Southern beauty was rebuilt into an 0-6-0T(tank) by the Spencer, N. C. "boys" and became the "Spencer Shop Goat" until it was scrapped at Haynes (Spartanburg, S. C.) in December of 1952.

It worked for many years putting in and pulling out the bigger "hogs" from the roundhouse—seen in the background.

Look how clean the Southern kept even this lowly "goat." The regular engineer assigned to No. 1595 had his name printed above the engine numbers: "O. R. Wagoner."

The Southern truly knew what the word "style" meant.

Both: Ray Carneal/Author's Collection

Coming at you as fast as its 56" drivers and track conditions will permit is a big, burly-looking Southern Railway System Ls-1 class Mallet compound 2-8-8-2 No. 4017 with 8 cars of coal and a caboose on a cold day in November of 1950.

The old girl, built by Baldwin in 1924, really had its local freight, possibly No. 60, making time on the St. Charles, Va.-Appalachia, Va. (22.4 miles) portion of the Bristol, Tennessee-St. Charles line-all part of the Southern's Appalachia Division. She had conquered mountain grades, sharp curves and inclement weather as it neared Appalachia; even through 26 years old she still cut a most impressive sight.

With a boiler pressure of 210 lbs., 437,000 lbs. of engine weight, the large "Malley" produced 84,350 lbs. of tractive effort. No. 4017 will be removed from the Southern's roster in November of 1952.

The Ls-1's & Ls-2's were built to do one thing on the road that "Serves the South:" work in coal (and mountain) service on the Appalachia and Asheville Divisions. Eventually several of them will be transferred to the Birmingham, Alabama area.

Notice the reinforced cowcatcher on No. 4017. This was done to help the 2-8-8-2 knock away rocks that might have fallen on the tracks or snow banks it might encounter. It was a ruggedly-built machine that did its job for the Southern, unrecognized and without celebration, up in the mountain hollows, away from any major settlement, carrying coal east and empty hopper cars west, day after day, week after week, year after year.

The Southern got its money's worth when it purchased No. 4017 back in 1924. That's for sure!

John Krause/Author's Collection

They may not have been the most powerful or fastest of the 1,000+ Consolidations (2-8-0's) owned by the Southern Railway System over the years. However, at least to me, the H-4 class of these versatile locomotives were the most handsome. A prime example of the H-4 class engine is shown here in Henderson, N. C. on the hand-operated turntable (note No. 390's fireman-on the left-turning his engine by "muscle-power") in August of 1949.

Why would I consider the H-4's as the most attractive and best sounding 2-8-0's to grace the rails of the Southern? The main reasons would be that I grew up with them! As a result, I may be somewhat biased to this class of Consolidations. Still, I cannot imagine a more aesthetically pleasing 2-8-0 class of motive power.

The Southern's East Durham, N. C. to Keysville, Va. line (88.1 miles in length) as well as the Oxford-Henderson, N. C. branch (13.6 miles long) were all part of their Richmond Division. For over 25 years, the motive power that dominated these lines included not only No.390 but fellow H-4's No. 385, No. 391, No. 400, No. 401, No. 402 and the older H-1 class (1901) No. 319.

Operations on these two lines by 1949 included two, daily ex-Sunday local freights. No. 67 traveled from Keysville to East Durham while No. 68 worked from East Durham north to Oxford (my hometown). It then made a round-trip from Oxford-the O&H Junction (a wye located 0.8 miles north of the Oxford station and in front of my house)-to Henderson. Once back in Oxford No. 68 would continue its journey to Keysville. Usually, No. 67 and No. 68 met in Oxford.

From the time of my birth in 1937, I watched in wonder and great joy the Southern's H-4's working "my" line; I even had several rides on most of the engines listed in the 3rd paragraph while they worked the Oxford area. Indeed, this "schooling" made me a graduate (with honors) from "Railfan" University!

No. 390 was built by Baldwin in 1907. It had 57" drivers, 200 lbs. of steam pressure along with an engine weight of 164,800 lbs. plus a tractive effort of 36,827 pounds and was hand fired-no stoker; she left the roster on March 4, 1952.

This photo was taken from the Henderson water tank. Just look at this beautiful machine: sleek, well-balanced, clean; her symmetry was perfect and, in my opinion, her appearance was almost as pleasurable as the far more recognized and famous Ps-4's.

I bet No. 390's fireman will be glad when No. 68 finally reached Keysville this hot, humid August day!

Hugh Staffort/Author's Collection

Southern Railway System's 3rd class freight No. 65 is shown leaving Raleigh, N. C., passing through the Boylan Tower area (just out of the photo to the right), crossing over the old Norfolk Southern's Norfolk-Charlotte mainline and entering the jointly operated (Southern-Seaboard) double track territory, which ran to Cary, N. C. (approximately 8 miles away) on its westbound trip to Greensboro, N. C. The next stop for the heavy Mikado operated train will be East Durham, N. C.

Ms-4-class 2-8-2 No. 4883 starts upgrade with 53 cars this September 15, 1949 at 1:30 p.m. After arriving from Goldsboro and Selma, N. C. No. 65 worked the Southern's Yard in Raleigh which was located between Cabarrus Street (where the Southern's passenger station was also located—now used by Amtrak) and the tower at Boylan.

The big Mikado, Southern's principle mainline motive power until the arrival of the diesel, was a Richmond built (1926) 2-8-2 and produced 59,600 lbs. of tractive effort; the 63" drivers gave the large but aesthetically pleasing "mike" good traction and speed with a respectable amount of tonnage.

I can vividly recall seeing No. 65 heading west out of Raleigh with doubleheaded Ms-4's. Now, that was a sight to behold! Two powerful 4800's, throttles all the way back on their quadrants, sanders going, stacks "shotgunning," bells ringing and a low, melodious and memorable steamboat whistle warning everyone to get out of the way. They passed by, showering you with cinders, shaking the ground, rods clanking—man, that was railroading in the grand style, a sight and sound (and smell) that hooked your author, making him a lifelong railfan and a great admirer of the Southern.

Ray Carneal/Author's Collection

When the first 2-10-2's appeared on the Southern Railway System in 1917, you could find them on both the Washington-Atlanta and the CNO&TP's mainlines; however, the big "hogs" were found unusable on the CNO&TP's "Rat Hole" Division. With so many narrow tunnels on this line, the 2-10-2's proved to be both too big and two powerful. The stack-blasting in those small enclosures knocked rock from their ceilings and the smoke and gasses the Santa Fe type engines produced came close to asphyxiating the crews. Fortunately, when the Ms-4 Mikados arrived, the 2-10-2's were removed from the "Rat Hole" area. The big Santa Fe locomotives also proved too slow for the hot Washington-Atlanta main and were replaced by the Ms-4 class 2-8-2's.

Even though unsuccessful on the areas mentioned above, they proved very efficient on the mountain grades in North and South Carolina, Tennessee, and Georgia. Eventually, it was found that the 2-10-2's were ideal engines for the Asheville and Knoxville Divisions, especially the Asheville, N. C. area-called the "Land of the Sky."

The Southern Ss-class 2-10-2's worked most of their lives from Asheville to Spartanburg, S. C.-the "Saluda Grade Route"-and the Asheville-Salisbury, N. C. run-the "Swannanoa Route." The numerous sharp curves, especially on the "Swannanoa" line, proved to be a real challenge for such a big and long engine (85 feet from cowcatcher to tender coupler). To surmount this obstacle, the Southern equipped a great number of these giants with "floating" front drivers in order to negotiate these curves found on both lines.

The renowned Saluda line was more familiar to railfans; however, the run to Salisbury was busier and just as scenic. There were seven tunnels between Ridgecrest and Old Fort, N. C. on the "Swannanoa Route." The huge Ss-class 2-10-2 No. 5066, shown here exiting one of these "holes" (Burgin Tunnel) in July of 1948, had green flags and carried several stock cars on the head end of its 45 cars.

No. 5066 was built by Richmond in 1918. It had 57" drivers, 200 lbs. of boiler pressure plus an engine weight of 378,000 lbs. The tender, which weighed 176,000 lbs. and carried 16 tons of coal and 10,000 gallons of water, had 33" wheels and was 28 feet long; the compact yet attractive 2-10-2 developed a healthy 74,000 lbs. of tractive effort-statistics which enabled this locomotive and its sisters to become perfect mountain maulers. They continued to battle the grades, curves and tunnels until replaced by GM F-7 diesels. No. 5066 was retired in November of 1951 after conquering the Blue Ridge mountains for 33 years.

I can recall, as a young man, seeing the big Ss-class 2-10-2's passing through Hendersonville, N. C. on the Spartanburg line. Those heading towards Asheville, after mastering mighty Saluda Grade, actually appeared, at least to me, as if they were "sweating" after their grueling confrontation with the 4.7% grade.

They were good engines and served the Southern well for over three decades.

Frank Clodfelter/Author's Collection

SOUTHERN RAILWAY SYSTEM

IV

In The Mountains

Even the passenger trains had to have help getting up Saluda Grade regardless of the fact that the varnish had fewer cars and less tonnage than a heavy, long freight. A case in point is shown here in this most dramatic photo. Southern Railway System's beautiful green and gold colored Ts-1 class 4-8-2 No. 1491, pulling No. 27, the *Carolina Special* (Charleston, S. C. to Cincinnati, Ohio) with all its might, had to have assistance from a huge and powerful Ls-2 class 2-8-8-2 No. 4050 which, as you can see, was shoving like he__ to get No. 27's 9 cars from Melrose to Saluda, N. C.—approximately 2.7 miles of a 4.7% grade (even a short section of a grueling 5.03%)—to complete its journey.

No. 1491 (Richmond built, 1919) had 69" drivers and a tractive effort of 53,900 lbs. while the brutish No. 4050 (Baldwin, 1926) had 56"

drivers and mustered 96,000 lbs. of t.e. Needless to say, this combination of power got the "pride of the road" over the hill.

Look at the area: ankle-deep in cinders, heavily sanded rails. Many battles were fought here against Mother Nature. Even though not as dramatic as the steamers, the modern diesels such as the giants of General Motors and General Electric really "talk it up" to this very day when they take on the mountain.

I've often wondered how it must have been for the passengers in No. 27's last car as that ponderous 2-8-8-2 shoved and shouted to heaven with all it had to give in order to put No. 27 into Asheville on time. Terrific!

Ray Carneal/Author's Collection

Like some behemoth from the Cretaceous Era, the Southern Railway System's mighty Ls-2 class 2-8-8-2 No. 4053 is shown straining, clawing and fighting for traction as it pounds up Saluda Grade with 35 cars dragging behind. The surrounding mountains echoed the shotgun blasting sounds of No. 4053's twin stacks which were spewing smoke and cinders skyward. A battle was being fought here this May 21, 1949 at 11:35 a.m. Signs of other thousands of similar battles lay all around: ankle-deep cinders on the ground, worn rails whitened from the tremendous sanding; a smoky haze surrounded the area on a clear, sunny day.

Saluda! To railfans, be they Southern or not, knew what the name implied. Not the town of Saluda, N. C. itself but the severe grade that all westbound trains had to master in order to complete their journey from Spartanburg, S. C. to Asheville, N. C. (66 miles); eastbound trains had to meet an equal danger descending the grade, trying to avoid a runaway.

For approximately 3 miles from Melrose, N. C. (the base of the grade), whose elevation was 1,494 feet above sea level, to Saluda (elevation: 2,009 feet), all trains had to conquer the steepest and crookedest, standard gauge mainline railroad in the United States where the grade averaged from 4.09% to a staggering 4.7%-a rise of 605 feet in nearly 3 miles! The grade was so formidable that the huge Ls-2 class articulated engines-the largest and most powerful steam locomotives ever to be owned by the Southern-were only able to lug 550 tons up the hill!

Using all its 96,000 lbs. of tractive effort and even more, Southern Railway System's massive Ls-2 class 2-8-8-2 No. 4050 (Baldwin, 1926) is shown down on its knees, pushing for all its worth to help get this westbounder upgrade to Saluda, N. C. No. 4053, a fellow Ls-2, 2-8-8-2 (Baldwin, 1928), is up front of this extra freight bound for Asheville, N. C. from Spartanburg, S. C. (66 miles), this May 21, 1949 at 11:36 a.m. Just imagine: 192,000 lbs. of tractive effort, two Ls-2's with a combined weight of 1,320,800 lbs.-all at 10 m.p.h. and barely keeping traction with the heavily sanded rails. This was a typical example of what it took to get 35 cars up and over Saluda grade-the steepest mainline, standard gauge railroad in the United States-during the glory days of steam operations. Such scenes are extremely difficult to put into words which properly describes the drama unfolding before us in this excellent photo.

Averaging between 4.09% and 4.7% (some sources maintain that there is actually a small section which reaches an astonishing 5.03%) Saluda grade is a 2.7 mile long part of the Spartanburg-Asheville line, starting at Melrose, N. C. (elevation-1,494 ft.) and ending at the town of Saluda (elevation-2,009 ft. above sea level). The westbound climb was so great that it humbled even the huge 2-8-8-2 to moving only 550 tons up the hill.

The surrounding area was ankle-deep in cinders, the sky had a cloudy appearance even though, believe it or not, it was a sunny day. Many confrontations had been fought here over the years. The grinding on the rails required them to be replaced far more often than normal, for the heavy 131 lb. ribbons of steel suffered a great deal of punishment whenever one of these "confrontations" took place.

Once at Saluda, No. 4050 would uncouple from the train, drift back to Melrose where, if need be, the tender would be reloaded (16 tons of coal and 10,000 gallons of water); the engine would be thoroughly checked and then the powerful articulated would be ready to help push a freight or passenger job up the grade, starting another "confrontation."

Even though such mighty diesels as SD-70's and 9D-40CW's still have a difficult time taking on Saluda today, their struggles pale in comparison when two Ls-2's started blasting their way up this impressive obstacle placed before them by Mother Nature.

Both: Ray Carneal/Author's Collection

Just down from mighty Saluda Grade, an Asheville, N. C. to Spartanburg, S. C. local freight is shown "resting" at the base of the grade, Melrose, N. C. in July of 1949, with 14 cars.

Southern Railway System's No. 4610, an Ms-class 2-8-2, built by Richmond, in 1914, would remain here long enough for its brakes and wheels to cool off and its entire train thoroughly checked. The engineer is shown looking over his Mikado as is the fireman (in background).

Why all this attention? No. 4610 just descended 515 feet of elevation in only 2.7 miles, dropping from Saluda, N. C. (elevation: 2,009 feet) to Melrose (elevation: 1,494 ft.). The local was covered in hot brake and wheel smoke when it reached the foot of the mountain. It left Asheville (elevation: 2,288 feet above sea level) early this morning and would arrive in Spartanburg's Haynes Yard (elevation: 875 feet) later in the day.

The Ms (M=Mikado, S=Superheated)-class "Mike" had 63" drivers, a steam pressure of 200 lbs., an engine weight of 272,900 lbs. and could produce 53,900 lbs. of tractive effort. The attractive 2-8-2 was retired from the Southern's roster in February of 1953-a casualty of the diesel invasion.

To the right of the "resting" local was a westbound freight with a huge Santa Fe type S-class 2-10-2 along with an additional 2-10-2 on the rear of the 31 cars.

Notice the front of No. 4610. Even with the dirt and grime you would expect on locomotives in mountain service, this particular 2-8-2 looks clean. The Asheville Division crews always used a judicious amount of white colored trimming and "TLC" on their engines than, arguably, all other divisions on the Southern. This extra care and love can explain, to a large degree, why Southern's motive power performed so well so many years. Indeed, the most modern steam engine ever owned by the Southern came from the builders in 1928!

Ray Carneal/Author's Collection

Local freights such as Extra 4618 West, shown here one mile from the town of Saluda, N. C. on May 21, 1949, usually required help getting to the summit of this nearly 3 mile long grade running from Melrose to Saluda on the Southern Railway System's Spartanburg, S. C. to Asheville, N. C.

Ms-class No. 4618 added to the cinders, which are shown drifting down the bank on the right of the hard working 2-8-2, as it struggled towards Asheville, serving all the customers on this part of the Asheville Division in the "Land of the Sky."

Even though No. 4618 had nearly 54,000 lbs. of tractive effort, it could not have reached Saluda (top of the grade) without the help of a huge Ls-2 class 2-8-8-2, No. 4050, pushing for all its worth on the rear of this westbound local. No. 4050, a product of Baldwin (1926), had 56" drivers, 210 lbs. of steam pressure and a tractive effort of 96,000 lbs. During the steam era, you could hear the two "hogs" blasting their way up the hill at least 15 minutes before No. 4618 crawled around the curve and came into view, fighting for traction on the heavily sanded rails. It was truly a sight to behold-a drama of steam at its best-taking on this famous grade, shaking the ground with every revolution of its 8 drivers, the engine crew working in perfect unison. Scenes such as this remain with you forever. The sights, sounds and smells of this moment simply enhanced an already memorable event.

Within a few minutes after Southern Railway System's Ms-class No. 4618 (2-8-2) passed by the photographer, upfront of a westbound local freight that was blasting and fighting upgrade, a much louder and deeper sound began to grow in decibels, even greater than that of the hard working No. 4618. It was a sound of a twin-stacked articulated, down on its knees, pushing on the rear of this local freight. The volume of its "stack talk" bespoke of a massive Ls-2 class 2-8-8-2, No. 4050-the largest and most powerful motive power ever owned by the Southern-doing what it did the best, exerting all if 96,000 lbs. of tractive effort to get this local to its destination. The drama unfolding before the photographer was almost indescribable.

Saluda Grade, approximately 3 miles of track stretching from Melrose to Saluda on the Spartanburg, S. C.-Asheville line, presented all westbounders with a 4.7% climb plus a short 5.03% thrown in for good measure. It was (and remains) the steepest mainline standard gauge grade on any railroad in the United States. All trains, freights (including locals) and passengers, required either a powerful Ss-class Santa Fe 2-10-2 or, in this case a 2-8-8-2, to push on the rear or doublehead upfront to get the job done. The surrounding ground covered with cinders and sanded rails were examples of thousands of battles fought here.

Once in Saluda, the helper would uncouple from its train, drift back down the grade to Melrose and wait to assist the next westbounder on its journey, day and night, day after day. It was the most dramatic action found anywhere during the glory days of steam operations. The action demonstrated here this May 21, 1949 at 2:10 p.m. was no exception.

All: Ray Carneal/Author's Collection

No, the train is not on fire. The smoke enveloping this descending freight, No. 156, is a result of brake shoes and hot wheels. Before leaving Saluda, N. C. (summit of the historic grade) brakes were applied to all of No. 156's 36 cars. By the time No. 4021, a Southern Railway System Ls-2 class, 1926 Baldwin-built 2-8-8-2, reached Melrose, N. C. (bottom of the hill)-approximately 3 miles from Saluda-the brakes were red hot and really smoking.

After descending 515 feet in such a short distance, No. 156 would have to wait at Melrose while its entire train was inspected and the brakes were allowed to cool off before it could continue its journey from Asheville, N. C. to Spartanburg, S. C., nearly 68 miles.

Descending such an obstacle as a 4.7% drop, day after day, required the engine driver's brake shoes to be replaced every two weeks. In some respects, descending Saluda Grade was more dangerous than ascending the mountain. In fact, the Southern installed two safety tracks between Saluda and Melrose to help prevent the damage that could result from a runaway. Unless the engineer of a descending train-both freight and passenger-gave a correct whistle signal, the switchtender who manned each safety track (the switches were always kept opened) would not line the switch for the mainline.

The massive Ls-2's were the largest and most powerful steam locomotives ever owned by the Southern; however, even with their 96,000 lbs. of tractive effort, the mighty 2-8-8-2's were humbled to only 550 tons when fighting up Saluda. The Ls-2's had 56" drivers, 210 lbs. of steam pressure along with an engine weight of 432,000 lbs. (660,400 pounds counting both the engine and tender.)

Two prominent smells surrounded Saluda Grade during the era of steam operations: engine and brake shoe smoke. This May 2, 1941 (1:10 p.m.) was no exception. Indeed, it would be several minutes before the "fog" created by brake shoe smoke dissipated from the area. Soon, however, this type of smell would be replaced by soot and cinders from a hard working 2-10-2 or another 2-8-8-2 giant heading up the mountain.

Mountain railroading at its best! There were two routes connecting Asheville, N. C. with the Southern Railway System's Washington-Atlanta mainline: from Spartanburg, S. C. (over Saluda Grade)-approximately 67 miles long, or Salisbury, N. C. (The "Swannanoa Route") which was longer-and busier-than the Saluda route.

The Salisbury line offered one of the most scenic runs east of the Mississippi River, especially between Old Fort, N. C. (111.1 miles from Salisbury) to Ridgecrest, N. C. (mile post 123.2). As the "crow flies" the distance between these two towns was 3.4 miles. To keep the grade for westbounders between 1.34% and 2.1%, it took the Southern 12 miles, by rail, to get from Old Fort and Ridgecrest.

Here we see local passenger train No. 11 pulled by a beautiful green and gold colored Ts-1 class No. 1490 (4-8-2) meeting through freight No. 56, powered by a huge Ss-class Santa Fe 2-10-2 No. 5055, in the pass track at Coleman, N. C. (mile post 119.2) at 1:35 p.m. in July of 1947-notice No. 56's train stretching around this "S" curve in the distance.

Can anyone possibly imagine such exciting action taking place as the scene depicted here in the Blue Ridge Mountains: the No. 1490 working upgrade with its 9 cars heading west while No. 5055 drifted downgrade with its long freight bound for Salisbury, preparing to reenter the mainline behind No. 11 and continue its eastbound journey.

Thank goodness there was a photographer nearby to record this moment on film so that we can all see the marvel of steam railroading in the mountains as it truly was. Looking at this photo, you can hear and smell and feel the action taking place here-and some wonder why railfans are so devoted to their love of trains! Here, in this picture, is the answer!!!

Frank Clodfelter/Author's Collection

The Southern Railway System's Salisbury-Asheville, N. C. line (141 miles long, on their Asheville Division) traverses some of the most scenic parts of the Blue Ridge Mountains, especially between Old Fort (111.1 miles from Salisbury) and Ridgecrest, N. C. (mile post 123.2). Although only 3.4 miles apart, "as the crow flies," the Southern traveled 12.1 miles between the two towns in order to keep the mountain grades between 1.34% and 2.1% for all westbound trains.

During those 12.1 miles you found numerous curves ranging from 12 to 14 degrees, spirals, high fills, grades and 7 tunnels. No. 11, a local passenger train running between Salisbury and Asheville, is shown leaving the first of these 7 tunnels west of Old Fort (called "Point Tunnel") on its westbound journey with 8 cars at 1:20 p.m. in October of 1947.

No. 11 was pulled by Ts-1 class 4-8-2 No.1490 which was built by Richmond in 1919, had a much needed 53,900 lbs. of tractive effort for mountain runs. It was colored green and gold along with a great deal of white trimming plus a beautiful steamboat whistle.

Out of a tunnel, onto a bridge, even though it took the Southern over 12 miles to travel between Old Fort and Ridgecrest, the great distance was worth it since it helped the westbounders to pass through the mountains with grades under 2.1%.

This photo depicts the quintessential action found in the mountains when steam ruled the rails: SPECTACULAR!

Frank Clodfelter/Author's Collection

It is hard to imagine but within a few minutes, the hard working Ss-class 2-10-2 No. 5055, shown on an Asheville, N. C. bound through freight, No. 51 (running late), will actually be on the tracks in the foreground (at the bottom of this hill) this hot, humid and cloudy day in July of 1947, (3:30 p.m.).

Using every ounce of its impressive 74,000 lbs. of tractive effort, this massive Santa Fe type locomotive works upgrade on this kudzu-covered high fill near Dendron, N. C., only 3.9 miles west of Old Fort, N. C.

The crew of No. 5055 was especially anxious to get their train to the lower level of this high fill since it was scheduled for a "meet" with No. 16, the *Asheville Special*, near Dendron–there was a pass track located just to the right of this photo.

When I took my first train ride through this area (on No. 21, the *Carolina Special*), I could not believe it when I looked out of my window, saw tracks below me and within a few minutes I was on those tracks, looking up the hill to the tracks I was just on!

The huge 2-10-2's and beautiful 4-8-2's ruled this territory on freight and passenger trains, respectively, during the steam era. It was an experience I will never forget.

No. 5055 came from Richmond in 1918, and continued to battle the mountains until the Southern retired the "old girl" in March of 1950. They were true mountain maulers.

All Southern steam fans will remember the 5000 series 2-10-2's with much affection.

Ray Carneal/Author's Collection

A portrait of raw power at rest waiting for another battle with the mountain.

It's May 21, 1949, at 10:00 a.m. Sitting at Melrose, N. C., on the Southern Railway System's Spartanburg, S. C.-Asheville, N. C. line, we see a massive Ls-2 class 2-8-8-2, simple articulated waiting for a westbound freight. This particular day Ls-2 No. 4050 had been assigned to helper duty.

From Melrose to Saluda, N. C.-approximately 3 miles-you found, staring straight "up" at you and all westbound trains, the steepest mainline, standard gauge grade in the United States: Saluda Grade.

Even though No. 4050 was among the largest and most powerful steam locomotives owned by the Southern and could produce a respectable 96,000 lbs. of tractive effort, it was humbled by the fact that it could only pull (or push) a maximum of 550 tons up this mountain grade.

This was the usual procedure for a helper engine: when an Asheville bound train-both freight and passenger-arrived at Melrose (base of the grade), a "pusher" engine was placed behind either the caboose or last coach. After a brake test, the pusher engineer would give the road engine crew a whistle signal and then off it went, as fast as possible, trying to build up as much momentum as the engines could muster. Once on the grade the speed dropped noticeably until the two "hogs" were down in the 5-10 m.p.h. range when the summit was reached at Saluda after between 15-30 minutes of combat. If the freight

was extra long, half of the train would be taken up the mountain and left at Saluda. The two engines then drifted back to Melrose. Then this dramatic action was repeated until the entire train was safely at Saluda. The helper headed back to Melrose while the road engine reassembled its cars into a train and headed to Asheville.

On occasion, two helpers would be required to get the job done (one upfront, one on the rear or both on the rear). During the war years, it was not unusual to find 3 helpers on duty (one in front of the road engine and 2 on the rear)-what a sight! What a sound!!!

By the late 1940's until the end of steam operations, one would usually find a big, fat, powerful 2-10-2, Ss-class Santa Fe type engine as a helper or helpers on Saluda Grade. As a result, having a huge Ls-2 class 2-8-8-2 as the helper this late in the steam era was a rare sight.

In this photo before you was a true mountain mauler: nearly 100 ft. long and almost 16 ft. tall. Its engine and tender (16 tons of coal and 10,000 gallons of water) weighed 660,400 lbs.; there were 16, 56" drivers, operating with 210 lbs. of steam pressure and was a 1926 product of the Baldwin Locomotive Works.

Impressive, powerful-the adjectives could go on and on. To fully appreciate this human-like machine, you had to be there, to walk around the "beast," to hear it roar into action, to feel the ground tremble beneath your feet as it passed by in order to truly realize just what an Ls-2 could do.

Ray Carneal/Author's Collection

A MEET IN THE MOUNTAINS!

The place: Dendron, N. C. on the Southern Railway System's Asheville-Salisbury, N. C. line (Asheville Division); the time: 4:45 p.m., August of 1947; subject: a meet between No. 16, the *Asheville Special,* and through freight No. 81 (in the "hole"), just west of Old Fort, N. C.

No. 16, the *Asheville Special,*" is shown heading for Salisbury, pulled by a beautiful green and gold colored Ts-1 class 4-8-2, No. 1492 (Richmond built, 1919), with 8 cars. Waiting patiently in the pass track was through freight No. 81, powered by Ss-class 2-10-2, No.5073 (Richmond, 1918).

Within a few minutes No. 16 would be seen on top of the hill as shown on the upper left side of the photo-the exact area No. 5073 traveled twenty minutes before.

Fills, spirals, curves, grades and tunnels were found on the Old Fort-Ridgecrest, N. C. section of this 141 mile long line from Salisbury, which had automatic block protection.

Just think, scenes such as this were repeated time and time again, day after day during the steam era.

The two forms of motive power shown here (a 4-8-2 and 2-10-2) dominated this line throughout the period of steam operations. The Southern would not permit 2-8-8-2's in the area due to the numerous curves which ranged between 12-14 degrees.

No. 5073 was retired in February of 1949 while the sleek No.1492 left the property in August of 1953. The Southern got their money's worth out of both locomotives. That's for sure!

Frank Clodfelter/Author's Collection

That's 378,000 lbs. of hard working Ss-class 2-10-2 passing over an obviously strong bridge as No.5058 works its way west towards Asheville, N. C. from Salisbury, N. C. with through freight No. 81 on a cloudy, coolish February day in 1948.

The Southern Railway System's Salisbury-Asheville line ran 141 miles from the Washington-Atlanta mainline in Salisbury to Asheville and the "Land of the Sky," as the Southern's publicity department called the area; it had automatic block signals for protection.

Soon the big Santa Fe will have its train near the French Broad River which parallels the Asheville yard area. The "big lady" was retired in December of 1951.

During the steam era, this bridge over Mill Creek near Dendron, N. C. felt the weight of thousands of trains pulled by 2-10-2's, 4-8-2's, 2-8-2's; however, today the biggest, most powerful diesels from GM and GE roll over its structure.

Just imagine the tales the old Mill Creek Bridge could tell, the battles it could recount, the differences it has felt under the flailing rods of massive steam power and the grinding of the new mountain motive power that occupies its tracks today.

Both: Frank Clodfelter/Author's Collection

A "meet" in Barber, N.C. (10.4 miles west of Salisbury) with the two premier passenger trains in this area, the *Carolina Special*, No. 21 and No. 22 (the Goldsboro, N.C. sections—both shown here—of the Cincinnati-Goldsboro-Charleston varnish). The trains split into No. 27 and 28 and No. 21 and 22 in Asheville, N.C. where it ran as No. 27 and 28 between Asheville and points north.

Two PS-4's, 4-6-2's (engine numbers unknown) are shown nearing the point where the Winston-Salem - Charlotte, N.C. line crosses the Asheville-Salisbury route. A wye was located in Barber; however 90% of the traffic kept the rails to Asheville very shiny.

Look at that sky! A "photographer's sky". One problem could have affected this magnificent scene in a negative fashion, however. On occasion, those impressive clouds could move over the sun at the exact moment you released the shutter on your camera. Fortunately, Mr. Clodfelter got lucky this mild day in June of 1949; his work gives us an excellent look at this event that occurred on any given day during the reign of steam.

Oh, to be in Barber with Frank this day!

The expression, "A picture is worth a thousand words," is certainly true when it comes to this photo of Southern Railway System's Ts-1 class 4-8-2 No. 1480, pulling local No. 11 between Old Fort and Ridgecrest, N.C. with six cars. Indeed, the dean of rail artists, Howard Fogg, made a painting, using this photo as his subject, several years ago—a portrait which was used on calendars and in at least two books.

One can easily understand Mr. Fogg's fascination with the scene depicted here. Just look at it: a clean, green and gold colored Mountain type steamer with outstanding white trim, especially on its beautiful drivers, exiting Jarrett's Tunnel—one of seven between Old Fort and Ridgecrest (note the volume of smoke in the background).

So that both the *Carolina Special* and *Asheville Special*—the two first class passenger runs on this line—could make good time, No. 11 and its eastbound counterpart, No. 12, stopped at nearly every station,

picking up and setting off mail, express as well as passengers making short trips.

Even though a local, No. 11 still rated a big, beautiful Ts-1 Mountain with its 53,000 lbs. of tractive effort in order to conquer the grades and curves it faced while passing through the Blue Ridge Mountains. No. 1480 looks far more attractive now than when it arrived on the property from Baldwin in 1919.

Alas, the 4-8-2 was scrapped at Finley, Alabama in August of 1953. Regardless of this fact, all was well in the world this warm July 1948 day when No. 11 passed by the lens of locomotive engineer, rail historian and photographer Frank Clodfelter. Thanks Frank, for preserving this wonderful moment forever!

Frank Clodfelter/T.W. Dixon, Jr. Collection

Southern Railway System

Durham, North Carolina

V

One of the many scenes associated with steam railroading is seen in this photo: an engineer checking his "steed" while at a station stop.

Southern Railway System's passenger local No. 14 is observing its daily stop at Durham, N. C.'s Union Station this June 12, 1950. Engineer A. B. Waynick was unaware of a photographer preserving his actions on film. Indeed, his inspection of Southern's Ps-4 class 4-6-2 No. 1390 represented a routine practice by all engineers at one time or another on their runs during the glory days when steam ruled the rails.

His clean, light colored cap and spotless "jumpsuit" gives testimony that things are going well with No. 1390 this warm 8:00 a.m. morning (dirty clothes usually meant that a great deal of work had been required in getting the "iron horse" to complete its assignment).

Within minutes, engineer Waynick will be back in the cab—the king on his throne—releasing the brakes and pulling the throttle back to get No. 14 moving once more on its Greensboro-Goldsboro, N. C. run with 6 cars tied on behind that green and gold colored tender which has, as you can see, increased its coal capacity by having the "boys" at Spencer (N. C.) Shops build up its coal bunker.

Both engine and tender are still clean even though the days of steam operations on the Southern were rapidly coming to an end as a result of the ever increasing arrival of diesels on its property.

Indeed, the diesels have relegated this "lady" to such plug locals as No. 14 after running up and down the Southern's mainline for over 2 decades, providing power for the *Crescent, Piedmont Limited, Peach Queen* and other varnish whose names were well known by all who watched the ebb and flow of passenger trains on this historic railroad.

No. 1390 came to the Southern from Schenectady in 1924 and continued working for the road that "Served The South" until it was retired on June 29, 1953.

Mr. Waynick was the envy of all young boys: he was a locomotive engineer on a Southern Ps-4. As the old song goes: "Who could ask for anything more?"

Ray Carneal/Author's Collection

A brief look at this photo would probably result in one suspecting that this was just another Southern Railway System Ps-2-class 4-6-2 with a passenger train at Durham, N. C.'s Union Station. True, this was a Southern Ps-2 Pacific; true, it was photographed at Durham's Union Station on a passenger run; however, this was not an ordinary passenger train-it was the "Blue Devil Special" (a football special).

During the 1930's and '40's, the Southern ran many football specials, including into and out of both Durham and Raleigh, N. C. On October 6, 1940, this "ballerina" of a 4-6-2, colored green and gold with a graphite-covered smoke box and gold trim around the stack and cylinders plus domes, as well as white-rimmed wheels, arrived in Durham with the Duke University football team, the band, the cheerleaders and several fans in 8 cars. The "Blue Devils" had played, and defeated Georgia Tech the day before in Atlanta, Ga. (notice the automatic train control device hooked onto the lead tender tuck so it could operate on the mainline south of Greensboro, N. C.). After unloading its "cargo," No. 1337 will head a few miles east to East Durham, turn the entire train on the wye located there and then head back to Greensboro.

This beautiful Ps-2 Pacific rolled out of the Baldwin erection shops in 1913. the dainty passenger engine had 72 1/2" drivers, 200 lbs. of steam pressure; the engine weighed 232,000 lbs. and No. 1337 could produce 36,872 lbs. of tractive effort. Its tender, which carried 12 tons of coal, 7,500 gallons of water weighed 152,000 lbs. No. 1337 was 67 feet long and nearly 15 feet tall. The popular Rushton trailing truck was seen under the clean and colorful engine cab.

For several decades, the P-class light Pacifics dominated the several mainlines of the Southern. Once the mighty Ps-4 heavy Pacifics arrived on the property, the lighter 4-6-2's spend the remainder of their days pulling varnish on the light-rail branch lines where they proved to be ideal motive power due to their light weight and pulling ability.

No. 1337 was retired in June of 1947. I can recall seeing this locomotive, as a very young man, in the Durham area, on one occasion. It impressed me as an engine with nothing but "legs" and quite petite when compared to the bigger Ps-4; but she was fast, had good stack talk and it was really pleasing to the eye. For over 30 years, the Southern felt the same way about these beautiful "little ladies." Then, however, came the unforgettable Ps-4's, "First Ladies of the Pacific!"

Wiley Bryan/Author's Collection

The location from which the photographer took this dramatic picture of Southern Railway System's *Carolina Special*—No. 21-departing Durham, N. C.'s Union Station was a tower where the operator controlled the street's railroad crossing signals which he activated when he saw a train approaching. This was a job I always admired. Imagine, getting paid to watch trains and simply cut on a switch to activate the crossing signals when a train came into view and then turn off the switch after it has passed—wow!

Unfortunately, the days of this and similar structures were numbered, for automatic crossing signals were being installed. Notice the strands of wire next to the main track (No. 21's track). So much for progress.

Be that as it may, the photographer DID get this great photo of No. 21, a train whose name is steeped in rail history, crossing Mangum Street heading west to Greensboro, N. C., at 7:35 a.m.; and eventually Cincinnati and Chicago, pulled by a green and gold colored Ps-4 class 4-6-2 No. 1368 on June 17, 1950 with 7 cars.

The engineer obviously wants to stay on time since he's leaving the "Bull City" (Durham) with a vengeance, working the 1924 Schenectady built heavy Pacific at full throttle. The sound was tremendous and, at the same time, wonderful!

No. 21 was the Goldsboro, N. C. section of the *Carolina Special*. Once in Asheville, N. C., it will be combined with the Charleston, S. C. section and together (as No. 27) it will complete the journey to Cincinnati, Ohio; and then, over the rails of the New York Central, on to the "Windy City" (Chicago).

Even though it's 26 years old, No. 1368 still shines from the early morning sun. The green and gold colors and white stripping are clean and demonstrate the aesthetic appeal of this renowned class of Southern motive power that made them a legend. No. 1368 ended her service on June 29, 1953 when it left the company that it served for so many years with class and reliability.

Oh to be in the cab of No. 1368 this beautiful day on our way west for an adventure we would never forget.

Both: Ray Carneal/Author's Collection

What an impressive line-up of motive power! There are four Southern class Ms-4, 2-8-2's (No. 4843, No. 4911, No. 4914 and No. 4855—each with their own cabooses) found at East Durham, N. C. this November 10, 1948, at 2:00 p.m.

They have all been filled with coal and sand, from the tower seen in the background, and cleaned up by the local hostler and engine maintainers at the East Durham facility.

Why so much power at this location? The answer: The Ringling Brother's Circus is in town and it required four complete trains to get all the equipment of the "Greatest Show on Earth" to Durham. It will also require four sections to leave the city as well. In 1948, all, and I mean ALL of the historic circus, moved by rail. As a point of interest, Ringling Brothers-Barnum & Bailey, after a brief flirtation with trucks, returned to the rails to move from city to city. They quickly learned that railroads still provide the most efficient and dependable service and continue to travel by train to this very day. The Greensboro-Goldsboro main track is in the foreground.

None of the through freights, "hot shots," not even the local freights, could move their tonnage and revenue without having their cars put together into a train. The job of assembling the cars into a string awaiting a mainliner to pick them up fell to the lowly, unglamorous and little noticed switchers. They worked day and night, in all kinds of weather in order to get the trains out of the yards, onto the mainlines and into the company's ledgers of revenue and profit—the life blood of all railroads.

One of those switcher or "yard goats"—one of the many nicknames affectionately given to these little but essential engines—is shown "doing its thing," making possible the trains that carried the nation's business in both peace and wartime, at the west end of the East Durham, N. C. yard on the property of the Southern Railway System.

The A-7 class 0-6-0 No. 1653, a 1904 product of Baldwin, is in the process of getting cars ready for a westbound freight this October 4, 1950 at 2:00 p.m.

With Angier Ave. in the background, No. 1653 does its work as it had done for nearly 46 years. Forty-six years old and still in operation!

And look how clean the little 0-6-0 appears. The Southern not only took great care of its glamorous Ps-4 class 4-6-2's but its 2-8-2's, 4-8-2's and even its switchers as well: white trim, gold colored letting and numbers; a tender that sparkled in the afternoon sun. Yes, the Southern knew how to care for and maintain all its motive power.

No. 1653 weighed 145,000 lbs., had 50" drivers, carried 185 lbs. of steam pressure and was able to put-out 32,710 pounds of tractive effort; it continued on the Southern's roster until June of 1953—a total of nearly 50 years of service. Can a diesel boast of such longevity? No way! The little engine could make a "snappy" and sharp stack talk when required to do so but usually it just "chuff, chuff, chuffed" along—just as pleasing as the sounds of a Ps-4 (well, almost).

We are indeed fortunate that the photographer took the time to record on film this little, hard working "goat" in its element, doing the dirty work, going unrecognized, making railroading possible. No. 1653 was and will always remain a beauty in its own special way.

Ray Carneal/Author's Collection

Coming down from Keysville, Va. is local No. 67. After a full day of working its way south through Chase City and Clarksville, Va. as well as Oxford (my hometown) and Butner, N. C., 2-8-0 No. 402 is nearing its destination: East Durham, N. C.

On the west leg of the East Durham wye, the little but speedy H-4 class Consolidation will soon enter the Southern Railway System's Greensboro-Goldsboro line and then back its train into the East Durham yard. The Seaboard's Durham-Henderson branch of their Virginia Division is shown to the left of No. 67.

No. 402, along with sisters No. 319, No. 385, No. 390, No. 391, No. 400 and No. 402, operated on the Southern's Keysville-East Durham line for over 3 decades. No. 68 would leave East Durham shortly after sunrise, work its way to Oxford, make a roundtrip to Henderson, N. C.; then, back in Oxford, it would continue its journey north to Keysville, arriving there from mid to late afternoon. Its southbound counterpart, No. 67, generally passed through Oxford, on its way from Keysville to East Durham, while No. 68 was on the Henderson branch—both trains running daily except Sunday.

No. 402, was built by Baldwin in 1907, had 36,827 lbs. of tractive effort along with 200 pounds of steam pressure; it had 57" drivers and weighed in at 164,800 pounds. Unlike most of the "H" series 2-8-0's,

No. 402 had its headlight in front of its smoke stack rather than the usual position—just slightly below center of its front.

After crossing Angier Ave. this May 9, 1951, No. 67 races toward its goal at 1:30 p.m. The crew is ready for a rest after the grueling, nearly 90 mile trip on this hand-fired, "rocking and rolling" 2-8-0.

I grew up watching these 2-8-0's working in the Oxford area. In fact, kind hearted engineers allowed me to ride in the cab of No. 402 and other 2-8-0's on several occasions while they worked Oxford, which was in the heart of tobacco country.

Speaking of Oxford, during the harvesting time for the "golden leaf," business was so brisk (usually August through November) that No. 68 would be pulled by doubleheaded 300 and 400 series 2-8-0's on numerous occasions. Now that was a sight and sound I will never forget!

During World War II they pulled trains loaded with German and Italian prisoner-of-war plus war material from Norfolk, Va. to Camp Butner (now Butner), N. C.

The little "H's" continued to work the "D" line of the Southern's Richmond Division (Keysville-East Durham) until the coming of the RS-3's and GP-7 diesels. No. 402 was retired on March 4, 1952 after giving the Southern nearly 45 years of faithful service. I still miss them so very much!

Norfolk and Western Railway

NORFOLK AND WESTERN RY.

Passenger Power

At 10:10 p.m. the night before this photo was made, Norfolk and Western's No. 15, the *Cavalier* (shown here near Shawsville, Va.- approximately 23 miles west of Roanoke, Va.), departed Norfolk, Virginia's Terminal Station. By 8:15 p.m. this very night it would be in Cincinnati, Ohio's Union Terminal.

It's near 7:05 a.m. on April 4, 1957. Fortunately, the heavy morning fog had lifted and sunlight had broken through the few remaining clouds, for No. 15 was on its way upgrade and working around this lazy "S" curve with a big, powerful, streamlined J-class 4-8-4, No. 604, at the head of its 12 cars.

Since the fog had left all the rails wet, No. 604 was using all of its 80,000 lbs. of tractive effort and a great deal of sanding to maintain its expected speed through this rugged section of the N&W's mainline (notice how much whiter the westbound tracks were as compared to the downgrade, eastbound tracks).

The large but aesthetically pleasing, streamlined 4-8-4 came out of the Roanoke shops in 1942. It had 70" drivers, 300 lbs. of steam pressure, an engine weight of 494,000 pounds and a tender that carried 35 tons of coal plus 20,000 gallons of water; roller bearings were on all moving parts-both the engine and tender-and No. 604's drivers were counterbalanced for speeds in excess of 100 m.p.h. Slightly over 109 feet long and 16 feet tall, the J-class 600's were the most powerful, non-articulated and/or booster fitted northern type locomotive in America and the pride of the Norfolk and Western.

With that cyclopean eye leading the way this early morning in April during a time when steam ruled the rails, who could deny that No. 604 cut a most beautiful sight, one of appearance and efficiency.

Look at all the cinders on the right-of-way. A great number of steam battles were fought in this area for many glorious years.

John Krause/T.W. Dixon, Jr. Collection

A mallet compound on a passenger train? An old Norfolk and Western Z1b-class 2-6-6-2 at the head of a local in Durham, North Carolina? The answer to both questions would be "Yes!"

Even though you would think such an event would qualify for a "Ripley's Believe It or Not" column, this photo shows just such a movement: a big, burly Z1b just in from Lynchburg, Va. with passenger train No. 37 at Durham's Union Station on October 30, 1943, at 1:45 p.m. what an incongruous sight: all this huge locomotive for a 4 car train!

Seeing a mallet heading a passenger run during World War II was not an uncommon sight since the Pacifics, Mountains and Northerns were all occupied on the mainline hauling an unbelievable number of civilians and especially military personnel during the frantic war years. As a result, any type of motive power available would be used to protect branch line assignments, including this 1918 Schenectady built 2-6-6-2, No. 1483.

As mentioned above, No. 1483 was born at the Schenectady plant for the Norfolk and Western and classified as a Z1a. After the World War I era, N&W's own Roanoke Shops upgraded the old Z1a's, making them more modern, more economical and called them Z1b's. The rebuilt 2-6-6-2's had 225 pounds of boiler pressure which helped them to have a tractive effort of 75,830 lbs. in the compound operation and 90,996 lbs. in simple— all operating on 56 1/2" drivers which held up the 440,000 pounds of engine weight.

The Z-class Mallet compounds—the N&W had 190 of the "sluggers" by the end of the "Great War"—could haul almost anything a yardmaster could assign them, including passenger runs; however, speed was not their forte since they were not built with speed in mind. Still, they got their jobs done as did No. 1483 which brought Norfolk Division's No. 37 to Durham and will take local No. 36 back to Lynchburg from Durham this very same afternoon.

Even the non-railfans took a double-look at such a massive engine on the daily 4 car train in the "Bull City" area.

No. 1483, which was finally scrapped in June of 1957, sits on the Roxboro Street overpass at the east end of Union Station with the tracks of the Southern Railway System's Greensboro-Goldsboro line seen just to the left of No. 37.

I think it would be safe to say that this old coal hauler looked "most interesting" at the head of a passenger train, much like watching an elephant pulling a small wagon!

RIGHT:

The Pennsylvania Railroad design is still visible on Class E3, No. 503 despite the N&W modifications to the front end and the tender in this view.

Waiting to take train No. 35 on a nice, comfortable trip to Lynchburg, Va, you can bet there are not many riders on board for the experience. The train would have only a few years before discontinuance of service. The 503 had even less time as the modernization and streamlining of the Class K2 locomotives was bumping the Pacific's from service on all but the most remote branch line trains. The 503 would be retired in May of 1947.

All: Ray Carneal/Author's Collection

Leaving a quiet Durham, N. C. Union Station, Norfolk and Western's local passenger train No. 36, heads north to a 6:30 p.m. arrival at Lynchburg, Va.'s Union Station on a cold November 6, 1949.

The track arrangement as seen in this photo is as follows (R-to-L): the "house track" (a freight siding), Southern Railway System's Greensboro-Goldsboro, N. C. line, a stub-end siding ending at Union Station, the N&W's passenger track and the Seaboard's line down from Henderson, N. C.

No. 36, shown crossing Mangum St. with 3 cars, will make its 117.1 mile long journey in 3 1/2 hours, stopping at such places at Roxboro, N. C., South Boston, Va., Brookneal (where it will cross over the Virginian's mainline), Rustburg and finally Union Station in the "City of Seven Hills" near the historic James River and the C&O's mainline. Between Durham and Lynchburg, No. 36 will make several flag-stops as well. Passengers on No. 36 will be able to make a connection with westbound No. 3, the *Pocahontas,* as well as No. 26, the *Powhatan Arrow,* on the Norfolk-Cincinnati mainline.

With its 62,920 pounds of tractive effort, K1-class 4-8-2 No. 113, built at the Roanoke (Va.) Shops in 1917, will not experience any problems with its 3 cars. No. 113 had 70" drivers, 220 lbs. of steam pressure and its engine weighed 347,000 lbs. For many years the K1's worked the mainline, pulling both passenger and "red ball" freights. With the arrival of the class-J northerns, however, they were assigned to branch line passenger and freight service.

No. 113 worked for the N&W for nearly 41 years until finally scrapped in June of 1958 as a result of the arrival of GM's GP-9's which flooded the property in rapid order.

With only a few minutes of rest remaining before its departure from Norfolk, Va.'s Terminal Station, we have an opportunity to view one of the most powerful steam locomotives, designed for passenger service, ever built.

The famous Norfolk and Western's J-class 4-8-4 No. 604 was built by N&W's own Roanoke Shops in 1942—a "war baby." When needed it could tap into its 80,000 pounds of tractive effort to conquer any grade and use its 70" drivers—which were counterbalanced for operations over 100 m.p.h. (something it did with great regularity, especially through the Great Dismal Swamps between Petersburg and Norfolk)—to really make time; and, with an engine weight of 494,000 lbs., there was little chance of losing traction regardless of the terrain.

No. 604 and its 13 sisters (Nos. 600-613) were the alpha of locomotive construction with every modern steam engine device available incorporated into its being, including roller bearings on all movable parts of the streamlined Northerns.

This particular J-class 4-8-4 had a unique distinction. For a few years, No. 604 was the only "J" that had a Franklin type "E" booster on the rear axle of its trailer truck which, during this time, gave it an almost unbelievable 85,500 lbs. of tractive effort when starting its train. No other 4-8-4 came close to having this much raw power. Indeed, some old class 2-6-6-2 mallets could not produce this tremendous tractive effort. Once the N&W realized its big, beautiful Northern did not need all this power, the booster was removed and No. 604 had to cope with only 80,000 lbs. of tractive effort like its sisters, with 300 lbs. of boiler pressure.

At 7:00 a.m. this August 8, 1949, No. 604 will take the 6 cars of No. 25, the *Powhatan Arrow*—N&W's crack passenger run—out of Norfolk and head toward Cincinnati, Ohio, 676.6 miles away, arriving there at 10:45 p.m. In between will be some of the most beautiful scenery one could witness: miles and miles of ancient swamps, mountains, grades, sharp curves, tunnels, bridges, etc. The ride for the passengers will also be smooth, comfortable, safe and on time. Even though the Norfolk and Western was known for mile long coal drags, what passenger trains it operated were first class since the road took a great deal of pride in its passenger service.

When the N&W decided to dieselize in the mid-1950's, No. 604's life was cut short, being scrapped in October of 1958—only 16 years old—a "teenager" in steam engine years.

The saddest sight was to see these grand ladies operating local freights on the Norfolk Division until they left the roster.

Thankfully, an entire generation of railfans were able to experience these marvelous machines in action with the numerous excursions pulled by No. 611 in the 1980's and early 1990's. No. 611 now sits in a museum at the place of its birth: Roanoke.

Thank you, Norfolk Southern Corp., for giving us one last chance to witness the J-class locomotive doing what it was designed to do: move the nation's public in a safe, inexpensive and comfortable manner.

All: Ray Carneal/Author's Collection

RIGHT:

Southern's westbound No. 75 is shown crossing Mangum Street and making an unscheduled stop near the Durham (N. C.) Union Station—its tower can be seen above the first passenger car—because of the Norfolk and Western train on the left!

N&W's No. 36—a Durham-Lynchburg (Va.) local passenger train—headed by 4-6-2 No. 559—pulls out of Union Station. The smoke from its departure can be seen in the background. Just as the local was leaving, Southern's Ms-4 No. 4853, pulling 52 cars, was also in the same area when No. 36 headed to Lynchburg. The fireman of the 2-8-2 looked back on his train and saw smoke. He immediately called "hotbox," so the engineer stopped No. 75 to inspect the long freight. It will be nearly 15 minutes before No. 75's crew figured out what had happened, i.e., the smoke came from No. 559! Meanwhile, the N&W local went along its merry way not knowing what problems it had caused. You can imagine some of the comments that were made by No. 75's crew about the N&W.

Ms-4 No. 4853 was built by Schenectady in 1924 and scrapped at Haynes (Spartanburg, S. C.) on October 17, 1952.

The track layout shown in the photo was (L-to-R): Seaboard, N&W, stub end siding, the Southern and the "house track" siding.

Leaving Durham, N. C. on March 21, 1953, Norfolk and Western's local passenger train No. 36 heads north on a leisurely journey to Lynchburg, Va., 117 miles away. It's 3:05 p.m. and No. 36 is due at Lynchburg's Union Station at 6:30 p.m. By this time the N&W was the only road still using steam to power their passenger trains in the Durham area.

Today's local is powered by K1 class 4-8-2 No. 113. The big Mountain type will not need all of its 62,920 pounds of tractive effort since it only had 3 cars to ferry to the "City of Seven Hills."

No. 113 has crossed over the tracks of the Seaboard Air Line (on the extreme right of the photo) and is now on the overpass above Chapel Hill Street with Durham's skyline in the background.

The Roanoke (Va.) Shops built (1917) locomotive had 70" drivers, carried 200 lbs. of steam pressure and an engine weight of 347,000 pounds. For years it held down mainline assignments until the 4-8-4 J class, bullet nose Northerns bumped them to branch line passenger and/or local freight service. Yet, it continued to perform admirably until retired in June of 1958.

Once in Lynchburg, the passengers on board of No. 36 will be able to head west on No. 3, the *Pocahontas*, to Cincinnati, Ohio since No. 3 will arrive at Union Station at 6:58 p.m.

On one occasion, the conductor allowed me to ride the rear car of No. 36 from Durham's Union Station—seen in the far distance background—to the N&W's engine facility, about 1/4 of a mile from this location. It was a grand adventure for this young man even though I had to walk about 1 1/2 miles back to Union Station after leaving No. 36.

Thunder on a crystal clear, cold morning in November? That's correct, for there was a great deal of thundering going on as we see a Norfolk and Western coal train taking on the 1.2% grade leading up to Blue Ridge, Va. on November 17, 1957.

Even with a huge, speedy, ultra-modern A-class 2-6-6-4 (No. 1237) and a monstrous helper in the form of a brutish, extremely powerful Y6-class 2-8-8-2 (No. 2150-the lead engine), the train's speed is down to a crawl with throttles wide-open, sanders on and both engines shouting at the top of their metal lungs. And that's not all. Over a mile to the west was an additional helper-another massive Y6-class 2-8-8-2 (No. 2139)—pushing for all its worth—to get this heavy train over the grade and on to its destination of Norfolk, Va.

Just think, scenes such as this were repeated dozens of time each and every day on this difficult grade between Roanoke and Lynchburg, Va. on the N&W's Norfolk Division mainline.

The usual procedure for this ruling grade east of Roanoke was for the helper or, in this case, helpers to cutoff after passing the Blue Ridge station area; the train's engine (No. 1237 on this particular day) would carry the coal on to Crewe, Va. and points east while the helper(s) would drift back down the grade to either Vinton or Roanoke, Va. and then wait for the next eastbound coal and/or through freight. Then the thundering would start once more.

Class A No. 1237 was built by the Roanoke Shops in 1949 and had 70" drivers, 300 lbs. of steam pressure; an engine weight of 570,000 lbs. helped to produce 114,000 lbs. of tractive effort. All moving parts had roller bearings and No. 1237 was equipped with every modern device of the day. The tender carried 30 tons of coal and 22,000 gallons of water. In 1953, the N&W equipped most of its mainline power with an auxiliary water tank (called a "canteen") which made an additional 20,800 gallons of H2O available. No. 1237 met the scrapper's torch in April of 1959.

The "elephant" of the Norfolk and Western, Y6-class 2-8-8-2 No. 2150, was bigger, more rugged than the sleek-looking class A No. 1237. The "workhorse" was built at Roanoke in 1940. It had 58" drivers, 300 lbs. of steam pressure, an engine weight of 608,460 lbs. and could produce 126,838 lbs. of tractive effort in compound and 152,206 lbs. while operating in a simple mode.

The rear helper, Y6-class 2-8-8-2 No. 2139, had similar statistics as No. 2150 although No. 2139 was built in 1939. Both No. 2150 (scrapped in October of 1958) and No. 2139 (scrapped: August of 1958) had roller bearings and were among the most efficient Mallet compounds ever built.

Concerning the 2-8-8-2's, an old N&W engineer once said: "When a Y6 got down to 6 m.p.h., just pull the throttle wide open and you couldn't stop her!"

"Blue Ridge:" in the waning days of steam operations it was like a magnet for railfans. With such scenes as pictured here, you could understand why so many of them journeyed to the area to watch and photograph steam action at its best one last time.

John Krause/T.W. Dixon, Jr. Collection

Norfolk and Western Ry.

Freight Power

With a Y6-class 2-8-8-2 helper (No. 2150) and road engine class A 2-6-6-4, No. 1237 upfront of this 170 car coal train, the Norfolk and Western assigned an additional helper, Y6-class No. 2139 (shown here), to add its muscles to the fight in order to get Extra 1237 East up and over the tortuous 1.2% grade to Blue Ridge, Va. where the summit would be reached and the fight against gravity and the mountains would be over. Beyond Blue Ridge it would be practically downgrade all the way to Norfolk, Va. and a waiting ship that would take all the coal from this train on a sea voyage.

The crew in the caboose on this November 17, 1957, must have had a great deal of confidence in the construction of their "crummy" since the huge Y6 had 126,838 lbs. of tractive effort (compound) and 152,206 lbs. in simple operation to help get the train up the hill. That's a great deal of power, pushing for all its worth, behind the apparently sturdy little "red car."

No. 2139 rolled out of the Roanoke shops in 1939 and by the 1950's it had 300 lbs. of steam pressure plus an engine weight of 608,460 lbs. Its equally massive tender carried 30 tons of coal and 22,000 gallons of water. It was scrapped in August of 1958.

You might have noticed that No. 2139 did not have a "canteen," i.e., an auxiliary tender (20,800 gallons of water capacity), tied on behind its own tender. Most helper engines did not venture east of Blue Ridge so there was no great need for extra water.

After the extra east was over the grade, No. 2139 would drift back to either Vinton, Va. or Roanoke and wait for another fight against the mountains.

The sounds were terrific! I wonder if the rear end crew had ear plugs? What an unforgettable sight! Even this far away from the action, the ground still shakes as a result of the 2-8-8-2's power.

All: John Krause/T.W. Dixon, Jr. Collection

Approaching the photographer was probably the ultimate of the compound Mallet Steam locomotive design in America, the Norfolk and Western's Y6b-class 2-8-8-2. They were the true "workhorse" on the N&W: the best mountain engine on their roster and a good performer in flat territory as well since its drivers were counterbalanced for speeds up to 50 m.p.h. Indeed, dispatchers always tried to save a Y6b for a time freight through the mountains. They also had clean lines and possessed a pleasing appearance which made one automatically think of an all powerful locomotive.

Powerful? This photogenic 2-8-8-2 could produce 126,838 lbs. of tractive effort in compound operation plus an astonishing 152,206 lbs. in simple. That's power!

No. 2189 is shown here pulling 155 cars of coal east near Williamson, West Virginia on May 18, 1955, with the assistance of another Y6b, No. 2200, pushing on the rear. The massive Y6b's had 58" driver, 300 lbs. of steam pressure plus an engine weight of 611,520 pounds. The engine and tender stretched to 114 feet 10 1/2 inches and stood nearly 16 feet tall. With the auxiliary tender ("canteen"), the huge engine had access to an additional 20,800 gallons of water which made it possible for the 2-8-8-2 to hustle by many watering locations thereby increasing its efficiency in

moving tonnage; with roller bearings on all moving parts-both engine and tender-you had an ultra-modern machine that could get the job done in less time and less cost than any other engine of its wheel arrangement.

The Norfolk and Western, looking at the Y6b's performance, actually had the blue prints of a proposed Y7 type 2-8-8-2 on the drawing board when the diesels arrived on the property.

Whether a Y7 could outperform a Y6b is a moot point; however, it was undeniable that the Y6b's were among the best of the best, even matching and, in some areas, exceeding the performance of 4, F-7, 6,000 h.p. diesel demonstrators from General Motors in 1952.

This was an excellent photograph depicting power and efficiency in action; the photo must have been made on the weekend since the motorcar, seen on the left, was not in use.

The morning fog had gone, replaced by beautiful sunlight, and you found one of the many dramatic bridges on the Norfolk and Western's Bluefield, West Virginia-Norton, Va. line. Now, as a photographer, all that was needed to complete the setting was a train.

Within minutes after starting to wait for a "subject"-one of the main tasks of a rail photographer (waiting)-there was a sound in the distance: first a "rumble," then a whistle-all approaching your location. Then, with a smile on your face, you saw it: an extra south mixed freight pulled by one of the most attractive N&W Z1b class 2-6-6-2's (No. 1479) on their roster this wonderful May 27, 1952. Now, the scenario was complete: beautiful weather, beautiful bridge, beautiful train, beautiful picture. Man, it doesn't get any better than this!

The old faithful Z1b was a product of the Schenectady Works

(1918). It had 56 1/2" driver, 235 lbs. of steam pressure, an engine weight of 440,000 lbs. and the 2-6-6-2 could produce 75,830 lbs. of tractive effort in compound operation plus 90,996 pounds in its simple mode. The tender held 23 tons of coal and 16,000 gallons of water.

Over 100 feet long and approximately 15 1/2 feet tall, No. 1479 had 33 cars (mostly hoppers) as it passed by with rods clanking, steam hissing, causing both the bridge and surrounding ground to shake and tremble.

This was one of the many dramatic moments of steam history that occurred each and every day. Fortunately, this particular drama was frozen in time by the photographer (thank goodness). Oh, believe it or not, the flags on the old "Z" were actually white!

Last of the Norfolk and Western's fabulous Y6b class 2-8-8-2's, considered by most as the ultimate design of the Mallet compound articulated locomotive in American railroad for power and efficiency, No.2200 is shown using its immense tractive effort to help get this 155 coal train, extra 2189 east-near Williamson, West Virginia-to its destination.

The Y6b's did not have the sharp "crack" of exhaust such as an A-class 2-6-6-4 when working all-out; however, its deeper stack talk would rival the A's in decibels of sound. No. 2200 has its sanders on (look at the whiteness of its first set of drivers) as it pushed the extra with all its massive power this May 18, 1955. The Y6b's were truly the "workhorse" of the N&W.

No. 2200 came out of the Roanoke shops in 1952, equipped with roller bearings on all rolling parts-both engine and tender; it also possessed every modern contrivance available in 1952 to make it the best of the 2-8-8-2 wheel arrangement. With the auxiliary tender (added to most mainline freight power in 1953), which contained an additional 20,800 gallons of H_2O, No. 2200's area of operation was increased noticeably.

The "grunting" of this huge engine (over 114 feet long and nearly 16 feet tall) was tremendous! The ground literally shook as this marvelous, human-like machine passed by, helping the N&W maintain its reputation of possessing three of the most efficient steam locomotive types ever built: the "Big Three"-class "A," 2-6-6-4's, "Y6," 2-8-8-2's and "J," 4-8-4's.

Unfortunately, this modern locomotive worked for the N&W only 8 years, being scrapped in January of 1960. This was an extremely short life span for a steam engine which usually ran 30 to 40 years or even longer. You can blame this tragedy on the diesel.

The citizens of Farmville, Va. had a very loud visitor passing through town early this particular morning in October of 1956. Even though quite noisy, it was a familiar "guest:" a westbound Norfolk and Western hopper (empty) train heading back to the mines with the accompanying thunder of 191 cars, pulled by a busy and immensely powerful Y6a-class 2-8-8-2 No. 2163.

Between Norfolk and Burkeville, Va. (133 miles) the N&W had an immaculate double track mainline. At Burkeville, the tracks split: one went through Farmville, heading towards Lynchburg, Va. and points west, while the other turned slightly south towards Green Bay, Va.-called the "Belt Line." The two tracks came back together at Pamplin, Va. (167 miles from Norfolk). The line through Green Bay was used mainly by the coal trains and most through freights since it was a nearly gradeless and very straight line unlike the up and down, curvy route through Farmville. Empty hopper trains and some westbound freights used the Farmville line, especially if the "Belt

Line" was occupied by a train. Of the two routes, the Green Bay area was much busier than the Farmville main although all east and westbound passenger runs went through Farmville: No. 25 and 26 (*Powhatan Arrow*), No. 3 and 4 (*Pocahontas*) and No. 15 and 16 (*Cavalier*).

No. 2163 was a member of the modern, efficient Y6a-class 2-8-8-2 "workhorse" of the Norfolk & Western, rolling out of the Roanoke (Va.) shops in 1942. The Y6a's were provided with a large Worthington feedwater heater which can be seen on No. 2163, just ahead of its second set of cylinders.

This was an excellent way to start a railfan's day: a massive Mallet compound with nearly two miles of hopper cars passing through town at nearly 30 m.p.h. For an unknown reason, No. 2163 did not have its usual auxiliary tender this particular day, so water would be a problem before the large 2-8-8-2 arrived in Roanoke later in the day.

Today, there are rumors among the Norfolk Southern Corp., which was created in 1982 when the Southern Railway System and N&W merged to form the current NSC, that the Farmville line could be abandoned and the "Belt Line" would be upgraded to handle all traffic. Let's hope that it's nothing but that-just rumors.

All: John Krause/Author's Collection

Talk about action! This photo personifies the best of heavy-duty, mountain railroading when steam ruled the rails.

A massive Norfolk and Western Y6a-class 2-8-8-2, No. 2167, is shown charging upgrade into Blue Ridge, Va. in June of 1951, with 188 empty hoppers heading west to the mines. The grade facing No. 2167 was 1.35%. Its sanders were on and the rail washers were operating; the fireman had the steam pressure at the "company level"-300 lbs., and the stack talk was tremendous. The decibels of the sounds were probably above the harmful levels for the human ear-wonderful!

To the right of the storming Extra 2167 West was the front of another Y6a on a heavy eastbound coal train that had just conquered the grade from Roanoke (Va.) to Blue Ridge. The coal train had help. In fact, the Y6-class 2-8-8-2, in the background, which helped the train up the hill had cutoff from the eastbounder and moved ahead to clear up and wait for the coal extra to continue its journey to Norfolk, Va. After the 150 cars of "black diamonds" left the area, the helper engine would drift back to Vinton, Va. or even Roanoke where it would wait to help

another eastbound train fight its way upgrade (1.2%), once again, to Blue Ridge. This type of action took place dozens of time each day and night and 99% of this dramatic work was never caught on film-what a crying shame!

No. 2167 was built by the Roanoke shops in 1942 (a "war baby") and it belonged to the super Y6 Mallet compound series that proved to be the "workhorse" for the N&W; it also proved, with each trip, that the Mallet was not just a beast of burden. Instead, it could be a most efficient, economically sound performer.

Within seconds, the lucky photographer who recorded this scene on film will be showered with cinders coming out of No. 2167's cavernous stack as it fought its way to Roanoke. After a few minutes, the engineer will ease off the throttle and begin working the brakes since it would be downgrade into Roanoke.

Look at that tremendous front end of the hard working Y6a-WOW! Just imagine the sounds, the excitement, the feel of this moment-WOW! And people wonder why there are railfans?!!

Y ou're looking at one of the most modern, most powerful 0-8-0 switchers to ever grace the rails.

In 1948, the C&O had Baldwin build a group of 0-8-0's for switching assignments. Shortly after receiving these modern "brutes," the C&O decided to dieselize. As a result, the Norfolk and Western purchased all 30 of the engines in 1950. They proved to be even more successful than the N&W anticipated. Indeed, the C&O's C-16 class 0-8-0's were so good, the N&W had their Roanoke (Va.) Shops to make 50 more between 1951-1953, using the same C&O specifications. The C&O's 0-8-0's were classified as S1's by the N&W while the Roanoke built switchers were called S1a's.

No. 270, an S1, is shown doing what it was designed to do in the Durham, N. C. area on October 8, 1953 at 2:45 p.m. The "short leg" 0-8-0 had a most impressive 62,932 pounds of tractive effort with 220 lbs. of steam pressure; their 52" drivers supported an engine weight of 247,000 lbs.

You can understand why engineer O. M. Strickland was so proud of his "hog," for it had outstanding performance; it was reliable and, for a switcher, it rode good as well. Indeed, the N&W got its money's worth from these ex-C&O switchers.

No. 270 continued to serve its new parent until it was retired in August of 1959. It was without a doubt that these "young"—only 11 years old—S1's had many years of service remaining in them; however, by the late 1950's, the N&W began flooding their rails with hundreds of diesel road switchers. Still, this October day in 1953, we see a perfect combination of man and his machine, in perfect "sync," doing their job in a routine fashion, not knowing that the winds of tremendous change were approaching.

Ray Carneal/Author's Collection

A familiar sight on the Norfolk and Western and today's Norfolk Southern Corporation: empty hoppers west and loaded hoppers east—like a conveyor belt. Coal was, and remains, the biggest single source of revenue on the N&W and, today, the NS. Once the coal was unloaded at Norfolk, Va., the empty hoppers were sent back-A.S.A.P.-to the mountains and the mines for more of the "Black Gold."

We find Y6a-class 2-8-8-2 No. 2163 pulling 185 empty hoppers west in this photo, which was made in October of 1950, between Bedford and Blue Ridge, Virginia on the N&W's Norfolk Division's mainline. When diesels invaded the N&W, you would usually find four or five GP-9's doing the job of this single Y6a-pulling almost two miles of hoppers to Roanoke, Va. and points west.

No. 2163 was built at Roanoke in 1942; it had 58" drivers, 300 lbs. of steam pressure and an engine weight of 608,460 lbs. The 114-foot long, nearly 16 ft. tall monster could produce 126,830 lbs. of tractive effort when operating in compound and a massive 152,206 lbs. when in its simple mode. Its huge tender carried 30 tons of coal and 22,000 gallons of water.

Soon the No. 2163, which was doing nearly 40 m.p.h. when this photo was made, will be down to 10-15 m.p.h. and shouting to high heavens as it worked up a stiff grade leading to Blue Ridge, Va. After reaching Blue Ridge, it would be downgrade all the way to Roanoke and sprawling east Roanoke yard as well as Shaffers Crossing.

The No. 2163 had roller bearings and continued operating for the company until it was scrapped in November of 1959. They were part of the N&W's "Big Three"-J's, A's and Y6's. The "hoot" of their whistle is still missed up in the mountain hollows where the Y6's constantly did battles with the hills, hauling the "black guts" taken out of the ground of the Blue Ridge Mountains, day after day, either east to Norfolk or west to Portsmouth, Ohio.

Their performance for the N&W proved, once and for all, that a compound Mallet could be an economically sound investment, for they combined brute strength with efficiency. They were truly the "workhorse" for the Norfolk and Western.

John Krause/T.W. Dixon, Jr. Collection

Although more at home on a time freight the Norfolk and Western's superb and renowned class "A" 2-6-6-4's also handled coal and hopper trains as well.

During World War II, they were even assigned to heavy passenger trains and could perform at 70 m.p.h. with a long string of coaches tied on behind-the 1200's could do it all!

It's near noon on June 3, 1957 as Extra 1214 West, with 175 empty hopper cars (a "hopper train"), was shown passing through Villamont, Va.-on the east side of Blue Ridge, Va., summit of the rugged 1.2% Blue Ridge grade that all eastbound trains had to face. The 1.2% climb was especially tough for the coal trains heading for Norfolk, Va. In fact, it was a grade where helper engines were assigned (usually a massive Y-class 2-8-8-2).

Many railfans were unaware of the fact that westbound trains had to tackle a stiff 1.35% grade to reach the Blue Ridge station; however, westbound trains usually consisted of mostly hopper trains and short time freights, so it was a rare sight to find a doubleheader going west. Still, with 175 empty cars tied on behind, A-class No. 1214 was "shotgunning" at approximately 10-15 m.p.h., passing a watering location which it will not use, for along with its regular tender (30 tons of coal and 22,000 gallons of water) the 2-6-6-4 also had an auxiliary

tender (called a "canteen" by the N&W crews) which provided an additional 20,800 gallons of water.

Speaking of No. 1214's tenders, look at the line along their sides which appeared to be drawn with a ruler. Since it was a rather hot day, the cool water inside the tenders left their mark on the outside of the hot metal. From the look of the water levels of the two tenders, No. 1214 will make it to Roanoke before taking on more coal and water.

The rails under No. 1214 were white-signs of the struggles faced by all westbounders. Next to Blue Ridge Station, this was a favorite location for railfans, watching the westbound trains fighting upgrade to Blue Ridge.

Class A's had 70" drivers (same as the J-class 4-8-4's), 300 lbs. of steam pressure and with an engine weight of 570,000 pounds, No.1214 could produce 114,000 lbs. of tractive effort. With roller bearings on all moving parts, the "A's" were truly the ultimate in steam locomotive design.

Such magnificent scenes were commonplace until the arrival of the internal combustion engine-the diesel. A great deal of romance left the rails when the "growlers" came onto the property.

John Krause/T.W. Dixon, Jr. Collection

You are looking at brute power, a locomotive designed to pull any and everything a yardmaster could tie onto its huge tender.

The place: Norfolk and Western's Durham (N. C.) Shops; the subject: N&W's Y6-class 2-8-8-2 No. 2143; the date: June 12, 1950.

There is no question as to the fact that the N&W proved that the compound articulated locomotive, if properly equipped and maintained, could be a success in moving tremendous tonnage in an efficient manner. Indeed, the Y6 class 2-8-8-2 was the first modern designed class of steam locomotive on their road.

No. 2143 had roller bearings on all axles; with 58" drivers. Standing nearly 16 ft. tall, the 2-8-8-2 was over 114 ft. long. Its tender carried 30 tons of coal and 22,000 gallons of water. The big Worthington feedwater heater is shown hanging over drivers No. 3 and 4 of it first pair of 2-8-8-2 wheel arrangement. Built at the Roanoke (Va.) Shops in 1939, this massive "elephant-like" engine continued to move tonnage for the N&W—coal drags or "hot shot" merchandise—until retired in January of 1960. The term "massive" comes close in correctly describing these engines, one of N&W's "Big Three," i.e., Y6-

class 2-8-8-2's, A-class 2-6-6-4's and J-class 4-8-4's.

No. 2143 came into Durham earlier in the day with a coal train (the dirty white flags, indicating an "extra" movement, still hang limply in their holders). The Y6 will journey back to Lynchburg, Va. this afternoon at the head of the daily through freight out of Durham.

Speaking of this daily freight, on several occasions, the tonnage was great and/or there were too many Y's in Durham and they were needed elsewhere on the system. Whichever the case was, two Y6's would often be assigned to the long northbounder. Seeing two of these "brutish" 2-8-8-2's coupled together, blasting out of Duke Yard, with the ground literally shaking beneath your feet, was an experience that would never be forgotten.

It might not look it but this Y6 was an efficient, modern steam locomotive that could actually hold its own with the diesel; however, by 1955, the Durham-Lynchburg line was dieselized and the "hooter" whistle of the Y6's could no longer be heard in the area—a sound and sight that was sorely missed.

Ray Carneal/Author's Collection

Scenery such as depicted here caused a great number of tourists to take a trip on the "Virginia Creeper" in the 1950's.

At a time when the Norfolk and Western had "diesel" on their mind but continued to rely mainly on their magnificent and modern J-class 4-8-4's, A-class 2-6-6-4's and Y6-class 2-8-8-2 steamers, they still had a few of the aged Mastodons at work on some of their mountainous, light-rail branch lines.

Shown here is the Richmond built (1906) M-class No. 382 (4-8-0) working on the Abingdon, Va.-West Jefferson, N. C. line in the summer of 1957, near the Hungary Mother State Park, south of Abingdon. No. 382 made a daily ex-Sunday round trip between Abingdon (which was located on the N&W's line to Bristol, Tennessee) to West Jefferson (55 miles away) as trains No. 201 and 202, and was nicknamed the "Virginia Creeper." It usually carried two Tuscan red and gold-lettered coaches, plus whatever freight was available, as its consist.

The nearly 51 year old 4-8-0 was still on the N&W's roster in 1957 due mainly to its 40,163 pounds of tractive effort, 56" drivers and 200,000 lbs. of engine weight were ideally suited for this light-rail branch line with steep grades, sharp curves and lightweight bridges.

Once mainline motive power, the N&W eventually owned 286 of these Mastodons—even when new the name, "Mastodon," made them sound old, as well as powerful—but, by 1957, only a few were left, No. 382 being one of them.

The Abingdon-West Jefferson line passed through some of the most spectacularly beautiful country east of the Mississippi River. During the 1950's, the public was becoming more aware of this fact plus the realization that a trip in this area would be behind a steam locomotive! As a result, both railfans and ordinary people were drawn to the N&W's Abingdon branch.

By 1958, however, the last M-class 4-8-0's, including No. 382, were scrapped and the "Virginia Creeper" became a part of history. Fortunately, with photos such as this one, we can remember the days when this "little giant," with its spark arrestor capped stack, prowled through the beautiful Blue Ridge Mountains bringing great joy to those who saw and rode behind it and creating memories that would never be forgotten.

John Krause/T.W. Dixon, Jr. Collection

Beauty and the Beast? Brute strength and speed? Utilitarianism and streamlining? Whatever the appropriate title may suit this occasion, one must admit: this was a most unusual power combination on this 198 car Norfolk and Western westbound "hopper train" on August 24, 1952, near Montvale, Va. Yet, this situation demonstrated one of the many reasons why a railroad's mainline was, and remains, so interesting: you never know what you might see, both in trains and motive power.

The photographer heard a westbound train approaching and it sounded like a doubleheader. Loud and quick stack talk was accompanied by a slower message of power on the move. Then, from around the "S" curve, emerged a massive and powerful Y6b-class 2-8-8-2 No. 2180. With its 58" drivers the photographer figured this was the source of the quick-pace stack talk and assumed the second engine was an A-class 2-6-6-4 since its 70" drivers would cause the slower-sounding stack music. He was wrong, for after the auxiliary tender (nicknamed a "canteen") of No. 2180 came into view, it was followed by a streamlined locomotive! At first glance, it appeared to be one of the N&W's famous J-class Northerns. However, as the second engine got closer, that big Worthington feedwater heater hung above the 3rd and 4th drivers revealed the streamliner's true heritage: it was a K2-class 4-8-2 No. 117 (N&W crew's called them "J-juniors" because of their resemblance to their bigger brother 4-8-4's).

What a grand sight, sound and comparison: the mighty Y6 "workhorse" of the N&W, stretching over 114 feet long and almost 16 feet tall, could produce 126,838 lbs. of tractive effort (compound) and 152,206 lbs. in simple operation. It was an ideal mountain engine and yet speeds of 50 m.p.h. were possible by this roller bearing equipped, ultra-modern compound Mallet, which was built by the boys at Roanoke in 1949. The K2, however, was another story. It was a dual-purpose 4-8-2, at home on either a passenger or freight train. No. 117 came from the Brooks plant of ALCO in 1919. After World War II, it was given a similar streamlining effect as the 600 series J-class 4-8-4's. The K2's, by the late 1940's until they were scrapped, were used on lesser passenger runs and were understudies for the J's if one needed to be checked by the shop crews.

Thank goodness someone had the foresight to record this unusual motive power combination so that future generations could see (1) that it actually happened and (2) just what it looked like.

Can't you hear the different cadence in the stack talk coming from that huge 2-8-8-2—the largest power on the N&W–vs. the streamlined 4-8-2 with its 69" drivers, 220 lbs. of steam pressure and 63,800 lbs. of tractive effort–both locomotives fighting to get the two-mile-long train to Roanoke, Va.? GLORIOUS!

Just 23.6 miles west of Roanoke, Va. we find Norfolk and Western's Extra 2176 West with 119 empty hopper cars west of Shawsville, Va., working up a 0.74% grade on March 21, 1957. Upfront of this mile-long train was one of the most modern and efficient Mallet compounds ever to grace the rails, Y6b-class 2-8-8-2 No. 2176 which was made at the company's shops at Roanoke in 1948-only 9 years old when this photo was made.

The fight ahead for 2176 would grow worse as the grade increased until it reached a grueling 1.34% at the summit, just east of Christiansburg, Va. However, 2176 would make the trip to Bluefield, West Virginia without a great deal of difficulty since it only had 119 cars.

It was not unusual to see a westbound hopper train with 200 or more cars passing through the area.

Today you could not take a picture from this location due to the grass and bushes. In 1957, the photo was possible due to the several inches of cinders on the ground which were spewed out of the stacks of thousands of locomotives working through this vicinity plus the fact that section crews-human beings-took pride in their assigned section of track territory unlike the mechanized crews with their machines which replaced the human touch.

The fireman had 2176 in fine form as it thundered its way west with slightly over 300 lbs. of steam pressure, resulting in the slight amount of steam passing through the safety valves and he just turned on the stocker which caused the smoke to appear from the hard working 2-8-8-2.

From this area one could see 2-8-8-2's on the coal and hopper trains, 2-6-6-4's on through freights, 4-8-2's on the locals and streamlined 4-8-4's on the passenger runs each and every day and night-those were the days!

All: John Krause/Author's Collection

This is what it looks like when 114,000 lbs. of tractive effort was being fully utilized-WOW!

Time freight No. 77 (from Petersburg, Va. to Cincinnati, Ohio) is shown near Villamont, Va. on March 21, 1957, with Norfolk and Western's A-class 2-6-6-4 No. 1214 pulling-for all its worth-65 cars westbound up the difficult 1.35% grade leading to the summit at Blue Ridge, Va. This was also the summit of another grade of 1.2% for eastbounders. The eastbound grade was the most famous of the two since the heavy coal and time freights required one and, on occasion, two helpers (usually massive Y6b 2-8-8-2's) to top the grade on their way east to Norfolk, Va.

The A's were more at home leading a time freight such as No. 77 although they could do it all (coal and hopper trains as well as, when needed, extra heavy passenger runs). The 1200's were as modern as an engine could be in 1943: 300 lbs. of steam pressure, 70" drivers (the same size as those used on the mighty J-class 4-8-4's), 570,000 lbs. of engine weight with roller bearings on all moving parts-engine and tender; they were almost 122 feet long and 16 feet tall. Their tenders carried 30 tons of coal and 22,000 gallons of water.

In an attempt to expand their range, the N&W began adding an auxiliary tender, called a "canteen," to its mainline class A's, as well as their Y6's-Y6b's, in 1953. These extra tenders made an additional 20,800 gallons of H20 available.

The ground was shaking, your ears were ringing from the shotgunning effects of No. 1214's stack talk, the speed was nearly 20 m.p.h. and the sanders were all working. This was truly a first class example of steam railroading in action! I'm sure No. 1214's fireman was thankful that he had an automatic stoker to help satisfy the insatiable appetite for its massive boiler. Fortunately, one "A" was saved from the scrapper's torch, No. 1218, which was retired from excursion service after 1994 by Norfolk Southern.

OTHER ROADS OF THE SOUTH   IV

Durham and Southern

Steam! Smoke! Thunder! With a combined 90,000 lbs. of tractive effort, two of Durham & Southern clean Decapods (look at No. 202's tender), 2-10-0's No. 200 and No. 202, are shown working upgrade out of Durham, N. C., nearing the D&S Junction where it will cross over the Southern Railway System's Greensboro-Goldsboro, N. C. line, on its way to Apex and Dunn, N. C. Extra 200 South has over 50 cars of coal brought to it from the connection with the Norfolk and Western in Durham.

The two Baldwin built 56" drivers 2-10-0's were using all their power this March 25, 1951, to move this tonnage. As a result of their effort the sounds produced were deafening and wonderful—all at the same time. The ground was actually shaking beneath the photographer's feet as 10 pairs of drivers fought to keep traction with the light rails and get its heavy train out of town.

The signal at the D&S Jct. (seen in the distance) shows "clear" so the two, hard working "decks" will not have to stop at the crossing—thank goodness!

The engineer of No. 202 is looking ahead and feeling his engine working, knowing from experience just how far back to pull his throttle without causing his drivers to slip and spin wildly.

Speaking of No. 202, it had the distinction of being the only new engine delivered to a U. S. railroad in the Depression year of 1933.

In 1954, both No. 200 and No. 202 were replaced by diesels—Baldwin built road-switchers—and the engines were finally scrapped in 1956.

This is a most dramatic scene, one that could only be produced with steam power. No one near Driver Street (being crossed by No. 200) could not help but stop whatever they were doing to witness this truly spectacular sight. This was a drama that was worthy of a Hollywood producer. It was a tremendous, unforgettable event!

Both: Ray Carneal/Author's Collection

LEFT:

With sanders on, the throttle all the way back on its quadrant, tremendous "stack talk," smoke shooting skyward, Durham & Southern's Extra 203 North enters East Durham, N. C. in a most spectacular fashion.

The extra north, pulled by a sleek, clean, Baldwin built Decapod No. 203, which was the prominent motive power on the Durham & Southern during the age of steam, is crossing over the Southern Railway System's Greensboro-Goldsboro, N. C. line and nearing its destination: Durham, N. C. — the "Bull City" (now called the "City of Medicine").

On the left of the hard working, modern cowcatcher equipped 2-10-0 are the tracks of (R-to-L) the west-leg of the East Durham wye, which was also part of the Southern's branch line to Keysville, Va., plus the Seaboard Air Line's track to Henderson, N. C. Approximately 20 cars back in the train—next to a telegraph pole—you can see the Southern's impressive coal and sand tower at the East Durham engine house and yard facilities.

Looking east, down Pettigrew Street, on the right, you cannot see the end of this extra north. Indeed, No. 203 had an incredible 45 cars of tonnage. Normally, two of the modern-looking D&S "decks" would

be assigned to such a lengthy train; however, only one 2-10-0 was available to ferry the extra, which had cars from both the ACL in Dunn, N. C. and the SAL at Apex, to Durham where a great number of the cars will be turned over to the Norfolk and Western (the D&S's main connection in Durham).

The 45,000 pounds of tractive effort and five pairs of 56" drivers are being tested with such a long, heavy train. No. 203 successfully completed its job due mainly to its experienced crew getting all there was to get from their engine.

Even looking at this excellent photo, it is still hard to fully appreciate the sights, sounds, the earth-shaking roar and emotionally charged scene unfolding before you this April 5, 1953 day at the D&S Jct. The term "awesome," which seems to be in vogue these days, does not come even close in accurately describing the feelings portrayed here. Keep in mind that such action was an everyday happening when steam was king—FANTASTIC!

Alas, in 1954, No. 203 and its sister 2-10-0's were replaced by Baldwin-built diesel road switchers and, finally, the "decks" were scrapped in 1956. The rail world was saddened by their departure.

Due to an extra large amount of tonnage delivered by the Norfolk and Western from their Lynchburg -Durham line, the Durham & Southern decided to run this extra south to get the cars out of the "Bull City" (Durham, N. C.) and on to Apex and Dunn, N. C. this cold December 2, 1951, afternoon.

The Durham & Southern was incorporated in 1906, with its main objective being to connect Durham with the mainlines of the Seaboard Air Line in Apex and the Atlantic Coast Line in Dunn.

As a result of its light rail and heavy tonnage, especially the occasional coal trains from the N&W (the D&S main connection in Durham), the 56.8 mile long road found the 2-10-0 Decapod-type locomotive to be the ideal motive power to get the job done.

In this picture, we see Extra 201 South approaching the D&S Junction in East Durham, N. C. as the two "decks" leave town with 45 cars. Both No. 201 and No. 202 are clean and capable engines and served the old D&S until replaced by Baldwin diesel road switchers in 1954. The 2-10-0's were finally scrapped in 1956. No. 202-the second engine on the doubleheader-had the distinction of being the only standard gauge locomotive delivered to an American railroad in the Depression year of 1933. The Southern Railway System's Greensboro-Goldsboro line, which the extra south is about to cross, can be seen in the foreground.

The 45,000 pounds of tractive effort and 56" drivers enabled these 2-10-0's to make good speed when the tonnage and track conditions would permit and they could lug tonnage surprisingly well.

This was a fine, busy little railroad that caught the fancy of railfans. It offered its customers personalized service and the crews were always friendly to those who admired and photographed its engines and trains. The Seaboard Coast Line took control of the Durham & Southern in 1976 and today both the SCL and the D&S belong to the CSX family.

The D&S became a part of rail history that is still missed to this very day. Thank goodness there were rail photographers who preserved the Durham & Southern in action on film so future generations of railfans could see what it was like, in this case, to watch two Decapods leaving town in grand style, a scene that only steam locomotives could produce.

All: Ray Carneal/Author's Collection

When one hears the term, "Mastodon," they automatically think of a huge, hairy, elephant-like creature that once roamed the earth several millennia ago.

The description of "huge" and "slow" certainly applies when discussing Norfolk and Western's burly M2 class 4-8-0's, sometimes called "12 wheelers" as well as the more usual term, Mastodon.

No. 1140, shown here working in the Durham, N. C. area on October 13, 1939, at 4:10 p.m. (the photo was taken from the top of a nearby box car), was built by Baldwin in 1910; it had 56" drivers, weighed 262,000 lbs. and produced an impressive 52,457 pounds of tractive effort.

The N&W crews found the M2's to be a fine steamer and very sure-footed in handling yard work, branch line duty and carrying mixed freights, especially on the many lines in the mountain areas; however, they were somewhat rough riding and "smoky."

Eventually, these 60 or so brutes, built for the N&W, were finally replaced by the 0-8-0 switchers in the 1950's—the last 4-8-0's were retired in 1957 and spend their last years on work train assignments.

In May of 1939, the power short Durham & Southern Railroad purchased one of the M2's from the N&W to do the work of a switcher—No. 1140. The D&S kept the number assigned to it by the N&W; however, soon after the arrival of the 4-8-0, the Durham & Southern decided on using 2-10-0 decapods to do the chores of both switching and moving their tonnage, so No. 1140 did not stay on their property very long. Still, while in service the D&S crews could not complain about the amount of tonnage the 4-8-0 could move.

No. 1140 was probably the most photogenic of her class with the white-trimmed drivers, graphited smoke box and stack as well as its overall neat appearance. Engineer Walter Williams seems very proud of his steed. Wouldn't you be?

LEFT:

Stretching 56.8 miles south out of Durham, N. C. to Apex and Dunn, N. C., the Durham & Southern Railroad acted as a conduit for many years between the Norfolk and Western (and to a lesser degree the Southern Railway System) in Durham to the Seaboard Air Line in Apex and the Atlantic Coast Line in Dunn. A majority of traffic was coal south, empty hoppers north; a good deal of general freight moved over its rails as well.

For several years, a team of decapods moved the D&S tonnage until the arrival of used, Baldwin built diesel road switchers, models DRS 4-4-1500 and DRS 6-4-1500's in 1962 and '65.

Two of the trim, clean Baldwins (1933) 2-10-0's, No. 201 and No. 202, are shown ready for action in Durham on January 8, 1947. They had 56" drivers and could boast of approximately 45,000 pounds of tractive effort; they could also make good time among the pine trees and sand through this section of North Carolina.

For the small rails and heavy tonnage, the high-stepping 2-10-0's proved to be the most effective motive power for this little road which is now part of the CSX family. Until it was absorbed by CSX, the Durham & Southern was a friendly, easy to like short line, offering what few on-line customers it had excellent service. In fact, during 1947, it operated 3 north and 3 southbound freights between Durham and Apex with one of the north and southbounders going all the way to Dunn.

During the age of steam operations in Durham, fans had the Southern's magnificent Ps-4's and N&W's K-class 4-8-2's to admire; however, many, including yours truly, thoroughly enjoyed watching the D&S's good looking 2-10-0's "do their thing."

Engineer E. R. Brewer has the trim Decapod of the Durham & Southern, No. 202, working up a slight grade out of Durham, N. C. This southbound freight, No. 11, is approaching the D&S Junction (the building on the right-background) where it will cross over the Southern Railway System's Greensboro-Goldsboro line (tracks at the bottom right) on its way to both Apex and Dunn, N. C. this May 24, 1953, at 12:55 p.m.

The 1933 Baldwin built 2-10-0 had 56" drivers and approximately 45,000 pounds of tractive effort. With the 75-80 lbs. rails and 32 cars, No. 202 will need all its tractive effort to not only pull its tonnage but to make good time as well.

The Durham & Southern provided the Norfolk and Western, coming into Durham from Lynchburg, Va., with a connection with the Seaboard Air Line in Apex and the Atlantic Coast Line at Dunn. As a result, a great deal of the D&S's revenue came from being a bridge route.

Within seconds, Mr. Brewer will open up the whistle as his "deck" powered No. 11 approaches Driver Street crossing. With the whistle blowing, the "stack talk," a moment in rail history was created: sight, sounds, and smells—all part of the steam era. Wasn't it all grand?

Ray Carneal/Author's Collection

With great fanfare and gusto, one that would please a Hollywood movie director, Q-class 2-8-2 No. 318-with its bell ringing-leads the southbound local freight out to Raleigh, N. C. on a beautiful morning in November of 1947-the huge coaling, water and sanding tower at the Seaboard Air Line's Johnson Street Roundhouse area is shown in the background. Ahead lies a great deal of work: sitting off and picking up cars, dodging Red Ball freights and passenger trains, before the Q-class "Mike" (Richmond, 1914) pulls its train into the big yard at Hamlet, N. C. The crew of the local will really earn their wages this day.

No. 318 was among the first batch of 2-8-2's received by the Seaboard-No. 318 was the last of the Q-class engines delivered. Over the years, its steam pressure was increased and the Berkley stoker was added to this previously hand-fired "Mike" (a real treat for all SAL firemen).

The Q's had 200 lbs. of steam pressure, 282,000 lbs. of engine weight, 63" drivers and a tractive effort of 54,700 pounds. Its Vanderbilt style tender held 17 tons of coal and 9,000 gallons of water. Although originally designed for the hot Hamlet-Richmond, Va. run, the Q's, in their prime, could be found on most principle lines of the Seaboard.

Can you picture a diesel-powered train leaving town with such drama, such action, such glory? The steam locomotive was one of man's most human-like machines ever produced. You could sense how it was performing by touch, by sound, by smell, even simply by the way it moved. No two engines were alike even though they belonged to the same class. Engine crews had to learn these idiosyncrasies if they were to coax their charge to operate at peak efficiency.

This type of action is sorely missed today in the sterile operations of the mass-produced diesels.

Wiley Bryan/Author's Collection

After working the yard at Henderson, N. C. Seaboard Air Line's Q3-class 2-8-2 No.398 is shown in the pass track with No. 97 (called the "short haul" by the Seaboard crews) waiting for a "meet" with Red Ball freight No. 80 in October of 1946.

Engineer Charlie Lynch can be seen in the cab while his fireman, Wiley Bryan, took this photo as the 2-8-2 waited to complete its journey between Richmond, Va. and Raleigh, N. C. on the SAL's Virginia Division.

No. 398 came from Baldwin in 1925 and remained on the property until May 25, 1955. It had 63" drivers, 300,000 lbs. of engine weight along with 200 lbs. of steam pressure. Its Vanderbilt tender carried 18 tons of coal and 10,000 gallons of water. The popular Q3 could produce 54,700 lbs. of tractive effort plus an additional 10,500 lbs. from the Delta trailing truck which carried a Franklin booster.

By the 1940's, the Q3's had less 1st class assignments since the R1 and R2-class 2-6-6-4's had control of most Red Balls and then came the diesels! Still, this late afternoon in 1946, we can marvel at the pump-loaded front end, low headlight, lean-looking 2-8-2. It had good stack talk, rode smoothly and was easy to fire which was good news for Mr. Bryan and his colleagues.

Along with the SAL's Decapods, the Q3 "Mikes" were the first steam power I can remember speeding through Henderson, N. C. (just 11 miles from my home in Oxford). They not only impressed this Southern Railway System fan, but the Seaboard as well since they were good, efficient engines and performed well for many years on the road that boasted that they traveled "Through the Heart of the South."

All: Wiley Bryan/Author's Collection

Two of the Seaboard Air Line's best on the ready track.

After being serviced by the Raleigh, N. C.'s Johnson Street Roundhouse crews, Q3-class 2-8-2 No. 450 is shown ready for a run up to either Richmond, Va. or Portsmouth, Va. this May 3, 1949 at 11:45 a.m.

It's companion was an F7-class 0-6-0, No. 1137. The F7's were recognized as the most efficient, largest, economical and outstanding engines of the 0-6-0 type ever developed in our country. These 0-6-0's had 51" drivers, 180,000 lbs. of engine weight with 205 lbs. of steam pressure and could produce 45,000 lbs. of tractive effort. Their tenders held 16 tons of coal and 8,000 gallons of water; No. 1137 was built by Baldwin in 1927.

It was 69 feet long and nearly 15 feet tall. No. 1137 would be ready for second shift duty at SAL's Johnson Street Yard this afternoon.

Q3 No. 450 came from Baldwin in 1926 and for many years, it was among SAL's main motive power. After the R1 and R2-class 2-6-6-4's (the 2500 series) were sold to the Baltimore & Ohio in 1947, the Q3's shared the mainline with the diesels until the internal combustion engines replaced all steam power in July of 1953.

What an experience it would be if only we could walk around Seaboard's Johnson Street facilities once more when steam controlled the rails.

Expedite! Expedite! Expedite! To get things to their destinations as soon as possible was the philosophy of the Seaboard Air Line Railroad from its inception in 1900 until it merged with the Atlantic Coast Line in 1967, forming the Seaboard Coast Line.

The SAL had to expedite the movement of both its freight and passengers in order to survive. Why? Look at its competition: to the East was the rich, flat, double-track high-speed mainline of the Atlantic Coast Line while to the west was the equally powerful, large and innovative Southern Railway System. The Seaboard was truly a "rock between (two) hard places."

Until 1935, the old reliable Mikados, usually doubleheaded, moved the preponderance of the SAL's tonnage. They did an exceptional job, especially the Q-3 class 2-8-2's; however, the Seaboard wanted an engine that could move more tonnage at a faster pace without having to doublehead its trains.

In 1935, Baldwin delivered 5 single-expansion 2-6-6-4 articulated locomotives (No. 2500-2504) to the Seaboard. Mention "articulated locomotive" and one would automatically think of a large, powerful and slow beast of burden-not the 2500's! Indeed, they instantly had a positive impact on the Richmond (Va.)-Hamlet (N. C.) run-254 miles: tonnage went up, speed went up, doubleheading became less commonplace. SAL was so pleased with the performance of the 5 articulateds-classed as R1's-they ordered 5 more (No. 2505-2509) form Baldwin in 1937. These new 2500's were given an "R2" classification.

Due to the influx of the diesels on the road that went "Through the Heart of the South," all 10 of the SAL's No. 2500's were sold to the Baltimore & Ohio Railroad in July of 1947, where they served for many additional years as their KB-1 and KB-1a class 2-6-6-4's (No. 7700-7709).

Shown here is Red Ball No. 80, powered by R1-class No. 2504 entering the Raleigh, N. C. area on a cold morning in February of 1943 after a night of a snow storm (yes, it occasionally snows in the "Sunny South").

No. 80 is crossing over the Norfolk (Va.)-Charlotte (N. C.) mainline of the Norfolk Southern RR at Boylan Tower. Soon it will be at the Johnson St. Roundhouse where a new crew will take this hotshot on to Richmond and a connection with the RF&P.

No. 2504 had 69" drivers, 230 lbs. of steam pressure and 82,300 lbs. of tractive effort; its engine weighed 480,000 lbs. and its tender, which was a semi-Vanderbilt type, weighed 301,300 lbs. when fully loaded with 24 tons of coal and 16,000 gallons of water. The locomotive and tender was 110 feet long and nearly 16 feet tall.

They were real "racers." Indeed, the Seaboard was the first road to prove that an articulated engine could be a speedy, efficient creature.

As a young lad, I can remember them slamming by the Henderson, N. C. station at 45 m.p.h. It was scary and fascinating-all at the same time!

A friendly engineer waves at the photographer as his 282,000 pound Q-class Mikado, with 31 cars, came at him doing 45-50 m.p.h. This was both thrilling, exciting and scary—all at the same time!

You might think that Florida was all flat land: no so. This photo, taken near Tavares on the Wildwood-Lake Charm Branch of the Seaboard Air Line, part of the SAL's North Florida Division (Orlando sub-division), showed the 1914 Richmond built Q-class 2-8-2, No. 312, coming out of a noticeable dip on this light-ballasted 70.6 mile long branch IN A HURRY!

One could tell that a steam powered train was at speed by the way the smoke from its stack laid back close to the top of the engine. This Q-class "Mike," nearly 37 years old, had its train really on the go. No. 312 was among the first batch of the Mikado or 2-8-2 type of motive power to come onto Seaboard property. The class Q's (No. 300-318) were designed to supplement SAL's P1-class Pacifics, H1-class consolidations and L4 ten-wheelers. Originally hand-fired, they eventually were equipped with the Berkeley stokers (a fireman's dream come true). They were also delivered from Richmond with Vanderbilt tenders.

By May 13, 1950, when this picture was made, there were approximately two through freights and a local operating in both directions between Wildwood and Orlando. A freight made a round trip from Orlando and Lake Charm when needed.

A light was attached to the front of No. 312's stack so, at night, the fireman could see how much smoke he was making and then make what compensations he needed to have a "clear stack," for less smoke meant a more efficient use of coal which the company wanted (it saved money).

Although not as powerful and popular as the pump-end heavy Q4's, SAL's Q-class 2-8-2's had an appeal of their own and worked for the Seaboard until the arrival of the diesel. It was finally scrapped on April 17, 1952—a sad day in rail history. While in operations, however, it gave a memorable thrill to all who saw them in action.

John Krause/T.W. Dixon, Jr. Collection

Sitting "in the hole" (in the pass track) in Henderson, N. C. is Seaboard Air Line's R2 class 2-6-6-4 No. 2507 with Red Ball freight No. 80 on a cloudy, cold day in March of 1942. Believe it or not, but No. 2507's fireman, Wiley Bryan, took this photo of his train as it waited for a "meet" with No. 107, the "Southern States Special."

No. 2507 came from Baldwin in 1937. It was part of the second batch of 2-6-6-4's (No. 2505-2509) that resulted from the fine performance of the first group of class R1-s (No. 2500-2504) that Baldwin delivered to the Seaboard in 1935. The single expansion articulateds had 69" drivers, 82,300 lbs. of tractive effort with an engine weight of 480,000 lbs.; the semi-Vanderbilt tender (24 tons of coal and 16,000 gallons of water) topped the scales at 301,300 lbs. when fully loaded and the engine plus tender reached a length of 110 feet (but could fit on a 100 ft. turntable).

The 2500's were different from any articulated ever made. Unlike most articulateds which were usually slow, powerful and ponderous, the SAL's R1's and R2's were fast, had good tracking abilities and could haul more tonnage than any other form of motive power found on the Seaboard's roster by 1935.

The "twin Pacifics," as the SAL crews called them, debuted on the hot Hamlet, N. C. to Richmond, Va. run of 254 miles. Soon, however, they eventually showed up on the lines to Portsmouth, Va., Charlotte, N. C., Atlanta, Ga. and Birmingham, Alabama; they ruled the rails until July of 1947, when, due to the arrival of diesels, all 10 of the fleet-footed 2500's were sold to the Baltimore & Ohio where, after a few modifications, they served the B&O for several more years.

On this particular day in 1942, however, we had an opportunity to look at this fine example of a fast and powerful 2-6-6-4 waiting to get back on the mainline and get No. 80 to Richmond and a connection with the RF&P.

Baldwin built them well and the Seaboard knew how to get the most out of these 10 "greyhounds."

Oh, to have been with Mr. Bryan when he got back on board No. 2507 to share in the "adventure" he was experiencing.

Both: Wiley Bryan/Author's Collection

This photo demonstrates the versatility of the Seaboard Air Line's Q3-class 2-8-2's. No. 345 (Schenectady, 1923) is shown passing through the Boylan Tower area of Raleigh, N. C. in October of 1946 with the dormitory cars of the Ringling Brothers Circus train enroute to the local circus grounds located in West Raleigh. Some of the Q3's were equipped with air signal apparatus and steam heat connections for handling either freight or passenger trains.

Extra 345 West had just entered double track territory (beginning at the bridge in the background) which was jointly operated by the SAL's mainline along with the Southern Railway System's Greensboro-Goldsboro, N. C. line. It continued to Cary, N. C. where the Seaboard turned south towards Hamlet, N. C. and Miami while the Southern headed west for a connection with their Washington-Atlanta mainline in Greensboro.

It's upgrade all the way to the fairgrounds so No. 345 will need all its 65,200 lbs. of tractive effort to get these 18 long and heavy cars to their destination. After all, the "Greatest Show on Earth" must go on!

With its heavy exhaust and sanding, the pump covered Q3-class 2-8-2 was putting on a most dramatic show of its own.

This particular location was, and remains, the best train-watching spot in Raleigh with (now) all Norfolk Southern-CSX and Amtrak action passing by.

Boy, that old and reliable Q3, along with its Vanderbilt tender, was really "talking it up!"

By March 1946, when this photo was made, this was becoming a rare sight-a doubleheaded steam combo taking on water-since the diesels were making deep inroads on the Seaboard Air Line's motive power roster.

The Johnson Street Yard in Raleigh, N. C. had enough cars to send a train to Richmond, Va.; however, there were no diesels available, so the yardmaster, who needed more room in his yard, took two Q3-class 2-8-2's from the roundhouse and sent them north as a solid Richmond extra.

The Q3 Vanderbilt tender only held 10,000 gallons of water along with 18 tons of coal. North of Norlina, N. C., there were a series of stiff grades, especially in the Bracey, Va. area. After fighting these grades with all the Richmond tonnage dragging behind, the two hard working Q3's "needed a drink" by the time they struggled into McKinney, Va.

The lead engine, a Schenectady built (1923) Q3-class 2-8-2 No. 355, filled its tank first; then the second "Mike," No. 401 (Baldwin built-1925), pulled "up to the spigot." Within approximately 30 minutes Extra 355 North became a moving light on the dispatcher's C. T. C. board in Raleigh once more.

For almost 20 years, the Q3 2-8-2's were the SAL's main motive power. They could produce a total of 65,200 lbs. of tractive effort (with the help of the Franklin booster-10,500 lbs.-attached to the Delta trailer truck). The 2-8-2's were 85 feet long and over 15 feet tall.

This was a scene repeated thousands of times each day when steam provided the motive power for American railroads. Within a few years, the water tanks were no longer necessary on the Seaboard since the diesels did not need a "drink" like these two thirsty Q3 "Mikes."

No. 401 was scrapped on August 25, 1953 and the same fate befell No. 355 on September 2, 1953-a great loss to those who loved the steam locomotive, the most human-like machine ever made by man.

Both:Wiley Bryan/Author's Collection

From the arrival of the first Q3-class 2-8-2 they became and remained the main freight power for the Seaboard Air Line until the arrival of the R1 and R2-class 2-6-6-4's and eventually the diesels. The first batch of Q3-class Mikados came from Schenectady in 1923; more Q3's were added to the SAL's roster from Baldwin between 1924 and 1926.

No. 442, pictured here between Atlanta, Georgia and Birmingham, Alabama (near Rockmart, Ga.) heading west with Red Ball freight No. 85 in April of 1949, came from Baldwin in 1926. It had 63" drivers, 200 lbs. of steam pressure, 300,000 lbs. of engine weight and could produce a total of 65,200 pounds of tractive effort (with the help of the Delta trailing truck which supported a Franklin booster that made 10,500 lbs. of tractive effort available) and its Vanderbilt tender carried 18 tons of coal plus 10,000 gallons of water. The Q3's were 85 feet long and nearly 15 feet tall.

The Q3's were larger, heavier and smoother riding than the other "Mikes" (Q-Q2-classes). They were the best of the Mikado-type locomotive on the Seaboard's roster even though the SAL acquired second-hand 2-8-2's from the Wabash in June of 1942-No. 480-487 (classed as Q4's).

The reliable Q3's (which eventually numbered a total of 117) could be found almost anywhere on the approximately 4,123 mile system. They had good stack talk and with the pumps upfront the Q3 looked husky but well balanced. In fact, they simply looked like mainline power and served the Seaboard well for many years.

I can still remember one incident as a young man when the family was out for a Sunday afternoon drive. We stopped in Franklinton, N. C. to get a soda. I heard the whistle of an approaching southbound freight so we headed for the station.

The highway crossing signal lights activated and, to my pleasant surprise, two fast-moving Q3's came into view with a Red Ball freight, doing at least 50+ m.p.h. The lead engineer had his goggles on, leaning forward with one hand on the whistle cord and he waved at this startled young man who waved back at this "god of the rails" with all the vigor he could muster.

What an experience! What an adventure! What a memory! Such an incident will live with me, with a great deal of pleasure, for the rest of my life!

Frank Ardrey/T.W. Dixon, Jr. Collection

LEFT:

While the fireman of this Seaboard Air Line Q3-class 2-8-2, No. 355, was getting water for his steed at McKinney, Va. in March of 1946, the fireman of the second Q3, No.401, took a photo of the action which was so commonplace during the age of steam. Once No. 355's 10,000 gallon capacity Vanderbilt tender was full, No. 401 would pull up to the "spigot" to quench its thirst. Then this solid Richmond, Va. extra would continue its journey north to Hermitage Yard in Richmond from the Johnson Street Yard in Raleigh, N. C.

The Extra North helped to provide more room for the Raleigh yardmaster. Even by 1946, there were still not enough diesels on the SAL to handle all train movements. As a result, two old, yet reliable Q3's were assigned this particular run.

No. 355 came to the Seaboard from Schenectady in 1923 while No. 401 was a product of the Baldwin Locomotive Works (1925). Eventually, there were 117 Q3's on the SAL; for many years, they were the main motive power for the road that went "Through the Heart of the South." They had an engine weight of 300,000 lbs., stood over 15 feet tall and 85 feet long. With a steam pressure of 200 pounds and the help of a Franklin trailer booster on the Delta trailer truck, the Q3's could produce a total of 65,200 lbs. of tractive effort.

With increased competition from the rich Atlantic Coast Line in the east and the powerful Southern Railway System in the west, SAL had to operate doubleheaded Q3's on occasion in order to expedite their Red Ball freights. The R1 and R2-class 2-6-6-4's and, eventually, the diesels bumped the pump heavy, muscular-looking "Mikes" from most of the mainline assignments until the SAL became all diesels in July of 1953.

This was a familiar scene in the days of steam, now long gone. It was missed by most railfans but not by the company who could see the diesel as their savior by the late 1930's.

Wouldn't it be great to climb on board one of these "mighty Mikes" and experience the drama as the two 2-8-2's got their train to SAL's yard in Richmond? It would be a truly grand adventure!

Soon the fearsome-looking Seaboard Air Line R2-class 2-6-6-4, No. 2506, will start downgrade to Raleigh, N. C., passing through the campus of North Carolina State College (now University-my alma mater) this cold, windy day in January of 1942, with 1st No. 82. In Raleigh, the single expansion articulated will be serviced and then a new crew will take this "Red Ball" freight on to Richmond, Va. and the RF&P connection. This section of double track, which extended from Cary, N. C. to Raleigh, was jointly operated by the Seaboard and the Southern Railway System's Greensboro-Goldsboro, N. C. line.

The 2500's were a welcomed relief for the SAL since it could haul more tonnage at a faster pace than the Q-class Mikados which had been the backbone of the Seaboard motive power until the arrival of the 2-6-6-4's.

The SAL was in great need of an engine that could not only move a great deal of tonnage but get its trains over the road at a much faster speed than their regular motive power. With the Atlantic Coast Line in the east and the Southern Railway System in the west, Seaboard could only meet this fierce competition by moving its freight and passenger trains in a more expeditious manner.

By July of 1947, the Seaboard had put their future in the hands of the diesel; they sold all 10, 2-6-6-4's to the Baltimore & Ohio RR where they served with distinction for several more years.

They were missed by the SAL crews for the 2500's could do it all: propel Red Ball freights, solid perishables, and even passenger runs when needed; they were smooth riders and could really "get over the road." One thing for sure: SAL proved that the articulated locomotive could be a fast, efficient and well-liked engine, not just a slow, powerful beast of burden.

At speed or at rest, the R1's and R2's of the Seaboard were a most impressive series of motive power

Wiley Bryan/Author's Collection

A "Russki" leaving town!

The Russian Revolution of 1918 was responsible for the Seaboard Air Line's first Decapod, 2-10-0 wheel arrangement motive power. They were built for Russia (by the Richmond Locomotive Works) which specified 5-foot gauge engines. The Revolution caused the United States Railway Administration (USRA) to stop their delivery, had the locomotives converted to standard gauge (4 feet, 8 1/2 inches) and made them available to American railroads. Twenty of these powerful engines were assigned to the Seaboard; they proved to be exactly what the SAL needed: 52" drivers, 180 lbs. of steam pressure, 207,700 lbs. of engine weight and 51,500 lbs. of tractive effort-ample power for light rail, branch line runs. The tall, thin stacks, huge domes, small drivers and large pony trucks were characteristics associated with the SAL's Russian 2-10-0's.

The "decks" proved so successful that the Seaboard eventually had 51 of the 2-10-0 types in their motive power stable. In fact, it was not until 1946 before the first SAL Decapod was retired (No. 515-shown here-was scrapped on June 16, 1950).

Mixed train, i.e., freight and passenger, No. 212 is shown leaving Durham, N. C.'s august Union Station with great bravado, pulling 19 freight cars plus one passenger-mail-express coach on the rear, heading for Henderson, N. C. on April 4, 1949. Before reaching Henderson, however, it will back into Oxford, N. C. (my hometown) from Dickerson, N. C. After working Oxford, No. 515 will head back to Dickerson and then complete its journey to Henderson.

The branch to Oxford went by my high school. Needless to say, my academic achievements suffered noticeably whenever No. 212 came into town. It made several long days at a school desk much more enjoyable, especially when No. 515's coal smoke drifted into my room. Those were the days!

Both: Ray Carneal/Author's Collection

Even at rest, Seaboard Air Line's R1-class 2-6-6-4 No. 2501 was an awesome looking steam locomotive. The big but sleek articulated was shown here in Raleigh, N. C. at the SAL's Johnson Street Roundhouse area in March of 1940.

The single expansion articulated type engine boosted the efficiency of the Seaboard to move more tonnage (and heavy passenger trains if needed) at a much faster pace. Until their arrival in 1935, the SAL relied on their Mikados, especially the Q3-class 2-8-2's, to get their freights over the road. However, as the competition of the Atlantic Coast Line in the east and Southern Railway System in the west picked up, the 2-8-2's usually had to resort to the practice of doubleheading to get their freight moved at a comparable speed with both the ACL and Southern.

Unlike most articulated engines which were slow, powerful but unable to meet the demands required by the Seaboard, the 2500's were built for both pulling power and speed. Baldwin sent the first batch of fast 2-6-6-4's (No. 2500-2504) to the SAL in 1935 (they were classed as R1's). No. 2501 and its sisters were 110 feet long (they could be handled on a 100-foot turntable, however) and almost 16 feet tall plus equipped with standard BK stokers (a fireman's best friend).

After this photo was made, No. 2501 had only 7 years remaining with the Seaboard since, by the mid-1940's, the road that went through "the Heart of the South" decided on the diesel as their new motive power. As a result, No. 2501 and the other nine 2-6-6-4's, (Baldwin sent the SAL 5 extra 2-6-6-4's, classed as R-2's, No. 2505-2509, in 1937) were sold to the Baltimore & Ohio in July of 1947. The B&O gave No. 2501 the number 7701 and classed it a KB-1.

After being serviced by the SAL's Johnson Street Roundhouse crews here in Raleigh, No. 2501 was ready for southbound Red Ball freight No. 87 which was due within the hour.

Every aspect of this human-like machine shouted: speed, power, efficiency! The 2500's were a breed of engines not seen before or after on the Seaboard.

LEFT:

The Russian Revolution of 1918 actually helped to introduce the Decapod-type locomotive to the Seaboard Air Line. In 1918 the Richmond Locomotive Works built a large batch of 2-10-0's for Russia; however, the Revolution stopped the delivery of the tall-stacked engines. As a result several American railroads took the 5 axle "decks," one of these roads being the Seaboard.

The Decapods proved to be an ideal wheel-arrangement for the SAL since they could handle a respectable amount of tonnage on the numerous light-rail branch lines which proliferated on the "Air Line" during its growing period. Indeed, the 2-10-0's were so successful the road had several more built. SAL also acquired even more 2-10-0's when they added more short lines to its family. Such was the case for No. 525, shown departing Durham, N. C. for a run to Henderson, N. C. with mixed (passenger/freight) train No. 212 on Dec. 6, 1949, which is approaching Ramseur St. (with the Norfolk and Western's connection track from their Duke Yard shown on the right).

No. 525 was custom built for the Georgia, Florida and Southern by Baldwin in 1924. The Seaboard took control of the GF&S in 1928. No. 525, which was numbered No. 402 when owned by the GF&S, had 56" driver and with a boiler pressure of 190 lbs. plus an engine weight of 212,000 lbs., could exert 46,510 pounds of tractive effort. The D2 class 2-10-0's were called "sport models" by the SAL crews since they were faster and more modern then their Russian "cousins." The "decks" could be found all over the SAL and continued in service until replaced by Alco-GE RSC-3 diesel road switchers.

Ahead for D2-class No. 525 are stops at Creedmoor, N. C., a roundtrip from Dickerson to Oxford (my home town) and then on to Henderson and a connection with the Seaboard's Richmond-Miami mainline. No. 525 left the SAL's roster on July 30, 1952.

The D2's had good "stack talk" when working tonnage "all-out" on the up and down Durham-Henderson line. I remember them well from my high school days since the line to Oxford went by my school; their arrival and departure in town was always the highlight of my days in the classroom.

This picture truly represents the Carolina, Clinchfield & Ohio Railroad, better known as simply the Clinchfield, in the days of steam operations: a huge articulated locomotive working upgrade through mountainous territory with a long string of hopper cars tied on behind a massive tender.

In 1909, the Clinchfield began operations, running coal south of Elkhorn City, Kentucky, where it made a connection with the Chesapeake & Ohio, to Spartanburg, S. C. approximately 280 miles away. In between these two points, the Clinchfield delivered coal to the Seaboard Air Line at Bostic, N. C., the Atlantic Coast Line in Spartanburg and, to a lesser degree, the Southern Railway System at Marion, N. C.

To move the coal through the mountains required huge motive power and the term, "articulated," became synonymous with the Clinchfield. Indeed, a group of massive, slow but powerful 2-8-8-2's became the major form of motive power on this rough piece of railroad.

The Atlantic Coast Line soon found that this coal road would also be an excellent way to get merchandise from the South to the midwest through the C&O's connection at Elkhorn City. Soon, mixed in with the coal drags and empty hopper trains, were several north and southbound through freights. The 2-8-8-2's, however, were not built for this type of work since they were too slow for fast freight assignments. As a result, in the 1940's, the Clinchfield took delivery of a group of powerful and fast 4-6-6-4's which proved capable of moving these non-coal revenue trains at a respectable speed.

One of these 4-6-6-4's, No. 661 (shown here), came on the property in 1947 and began blasting up and down the hilly line. They were smooth riding and, although they could not lug tonnage like the 2-8-8-2's, they got the job done and continued to roam through the hills, tunnels and up the numerous grades until replaced by diesels.

This photo, taken on August 3, 1952, at 1:00 p.m., shows extra 661 north working upgrade with an empty hopper train at Ridge, N. C. near Blue Ridge Tunnel and the Blue Ridge Parkway. Altapass will be at the other end of the tunnel. Between Marion and Altapass the elevation reaches 2,630 feet elevation, the second highest mainline crossing of the Appalachian Mountain chain.

This big, capped-stack 4-6-6-4, No. 661, had 101,000 pounds of tractive effort, 265 lbs. of boiler pressure, 69" drivers, 607,000 lbs. of engine weight plus a massive rectangular-shaped tender which weighed 397,000 lbs. and carried 26 tons of coal and 23,000 gallons of water.

Today, the CSX, which absorbed the Clinchfield, continues to operate coal and through freights, as well as piggyback trains, on this strategic, heavy rail, thick ballasted C.T.C. equipped photogenic line. Huge GE and GM six-axle diesels now do the job once done by the old 2-8-8-2's and 4-6-6-4's.

Now that the ex-Clinchfield is a modern piece of railroad, no one longer hears the blasting of mallets fighting the mountains. Instead, the roar of the biggest diesels made fill the hills and valleys. It's progress but it's still not, nor will it ever be, the same.

Ray Carneal/Author's Collection

Clinchfield

After completing an inspection of this through freight and running a brake test, the headend brakeman is shown climbing onboard this huge and powerful Clinchfield Railroad's Challenger type 4-6-6-4 as it leaves Erwin, Tennessee, heading for Elkhorn City, Kentucky on June 7, 1950.

If you think Clinchfield's No. 670 looks like a Union Pacific's 3900 series 4-6-6-4, you would be correct. During World War II the War Assets Administration (W. A. A.) ordered a group of 4-6-6-4's for the UP from the American Locomotive Works in 1943. Due to a severe power shortage on the Rio Grande, six of the Challengers were diverted to the D&RGW by the W. A. A. They were numbered in the 3800 series. At war's end the Rio Grande did not need all the power it had accumulated so, in 1947, six of these Challengers (No. 3800-3805) were sold to the Clinchfield which number them No. 670-674.

The Challengers, "War Babies" as some called them, proved invaluable to the Clinchfield which, before their arrival, had to rely on their slow, ponderous and aging 2-8-8-2's as their main power. The 4-6-6-4 could not only lug the coal—the main purpose for the construction of the Clinchfield—they could also make good time with merchandise as well.

The Clinchfield, now part of the CSX and C.T.C. operated, remains a busy conduit from the south to the mid-west, carrying a great deal of interchange between Spartanburg, S. C. (connecting with the ACL, Southern and the Piedmont & Northern) and Elkhorn City, Ky. for a connection with the C&O—all on an approximately 280 mile long road through the heart of the Appalachian mountains. Indeed, sharp curves, stiff grades, tunnels and other obstacles had to be overcome for the Clinchfield to move its tonnage. So, not only coal drags but hotshot freights prowled the heavy rail, thick ballast mainline; the 4-6-6-4's could outperform the old 2-8-8-2's and proved to be a great investment for the railroad.

No. 670 was built to UP specifications: it had 69" drivers, produced 101,000 lbs. of tractive effort, carried an engine weight of 607,000 pounds while the tender (26 tons of coal and 23,000 gallons of water) weighed 397,000 lbs. And the Challengers dominated the Clinchfield until replaced by GM's F-7's and GP-7's in the mid to late 1950s.

It was a most spectacular sight watching these massive and yet sleek, simple articulated locomotives taking on the mountains with all the furry and sounds that must have caused the gods of railroading to stop whatever they were doing to watch "the show."

Ray Carneal/Author's Collection

Short-legged, pump-heavy smokebox, large sand dome: this is a picture of a locomotive that conveys one impression: mountains! This is the Clinchfield 2-8-2, No. 414.

Running 276.9 miles from Elkhorn City, Kentucky to Spartanburg, S. C., the Clinchfield began operations in 1909 with its main reason for existence being to move coal out of the Appalachian mountain range to the Seaboard Air Line in Bostic, N. C., the Southern Railway System in Marion, N. C. and the Atlantic Coast Line in Spartanburg.

To manage this herculean task required a stable of huge, powerful, albeit not too fast, motive power, mainly 2-8-8-2's with tremendous tractive effort as well as 4-6-6-4's which came on the property during World War II.

Even the non-articulated locomotives had to be of excessive strength to cope with the grades, curves, tunnels and all the other obstacles the mountains presented the Clinchfield. An example of the "smaller" power is seen here, at rest, in Spruce Pine, N. C. (94.2 miles north of Spartanburg). Every item that would enhance the pulling power of the Mikado is in evidence. You would not recognize No.414 when comparing its builder's photo to this picture which was made on August 3, 1952, at 12:05 p.m.

Look at the location of its headlight; that beautiful and efficient Delta trailing truck. The bell was placed behind the smokestack since there was no room for it up front.

The 2-8-2's such as No. 414 were used in both yard and local freight work while the 2-8-8-2's handled the heavy coal drags and the 4-6-6-4's usually powered the through freights between the ACL in Spartanburg and the C&O in Elkhorn City. The arrival of the diesels in the 1950's eventually ended the blasting "stack talk" and the "hooting" of the steam engine's whistles throughout the mountains-a great loss.

The CSX, which placed the Clinchfield into its large "family" in 1987 (SCL, L&N, C&O, B&O, RF&P, etc.), has made the old coal road a most strategic part of its system. The line between Spartanburg and Elkhorn City sees not only coal trains but freights and piggybacks as well. However, the romance of the old Clinchfield has gone. It's just a railroad now, impersonal, rather than the line I remember which was friendly and exciting. It had a charm and personality that has evaporated into a giant corporation.

Both: Ray Carneal/Author's Collection

Originally built to haul coal out of the Appalachian Mountain range, the Clinchfield was approximately 280 miles of the most rugged mountain railroad you could find anywhere east or west of the Mississippi River.

To lug the "black gold" over this type of topography required power, not your 2-8-2's or any type of 4-axle engines, but REAL power. As a result, for many years the Clinchfield relied on huge, ponderous 2-8-8-2 compound articulateds. They were not fast but the monstrous size mountain maulers got the job done.

Eventually, the Clinchfield began to diversify. Using its connections in Spartanburg it became a bridge line for traffic from the South to the mid-west and vice versa.

Soon "hot shot" through freights began to move around the many coal drags and hopper trains, increasing the volume of traffic on this single track line. Eventually, C.T.C., long and frequent pass tracks (about one every 8 miles or so), heavy rails set in thick ballast made the old Clinchfield a "hot" piece of railroad.

The 2-8-8-2's and "stubby wheeled" 2-8-2's, similar to the one shown here (No. 499) at Erwin, Tennessee in between assignments on July 7, 1950, could not handle the "hot shots" because of their lack of speed. By 1943, however, a group of 4-6-6-4 Challengers arrived on the property and they provided the answers to the Clinchfield's problems for they could handle the coal trains and still make time with a block of Florida oranges.

Today the name "Clinchfield" is gone; however, the line is busier than ever in the CSX family. Indeed, you will find a great variety of traffic moving over the former CRR pulled by the most powerful and most modern diesels made by both GM and GE; however, coal remains the No. 1 revenue maker, helping to keep the rails both hot and shiny.

The Clinchfield: a most interesting, short and busy railroad then and now!

OTHER ROADS OF THE SOUTH
Louisville and Nashville

The modern era of superpower steam on the Louisville and Nashville was represented by the M-1 Class 2-8-4. The first fourteen locomotives arrived on the railroad during the summer and fall of 1942 and could not have come at a better time with the heavy wartime tonnage. The M-1's were originally assigned to the Cincinnati Division between DeCoursey (Cincinnati) and Corbin, Kentucky, they gave a new meaning to "fast freight" on the L&N. The tractive effort was calculated at 65,290 lbs and the locomotives quickly became operating crew favorites.

The big engines were never known as "berkshires" on the L&N, instead, they were nicknamed by the crews "Big Emmas." The railroad was pleased with the "Big Emma's" and ordered and additional six in 1944, and another twenty-two in 1948. Four locomotives of the initial order were equipped for passenger service, and handled the heavy wartime consists of the *Southland* and *Flamingo* on the Cincinnati-Corbin route as well as freight.

In June of 1954, one of the original order from Baldwin, No. 1962 leads a train of empty hoppers out of Decoursey Yard on their way back to the eastern Kentucky mines. The Cincinnati and Eastern Kentucky (EK) divisions were the last stronghold of steam on the L&N.

Edison H. Thompson/L&N Collection/U of L Archives

Heavy passenger traffic and year-round Florida trains caused the Louisville and Nashville to look for heavier passenger power in the mid-1920's. The Pacifics simply were not heavy enough to handle the large, heavy trains, in 1926 fourteen of the L-1 Class 4-8-2s were received from Baldwin, six more were ordered in 1930. Based on the USRA light Mountain, the road was quite happy with the locomotives and they spent most of their service on the Cincinnati to Atlanta, Ga. and Cincinnati to Birmingham, Alabama routes.

Alas, the arrival of E-units beginning in 1942 sent the L-1's to the lesser passenger trains and finally ended their service life in fast freight service.

The first of the order, No. 400 is dressed up with the standard L&N paint scheme, black with imitation gold lettering. The 400 is decked out with silvered pony truck hubs, cylinder heads and driver centers and running boards. L&N's passenger power was also adorned with a red and gold L&N herald painted on the side of the cab. This view was made at Radnor Yard in Nashville Tenn in 1936 showing the care crews lavished on the motive power in the days before the diesels arrived.

At left, things were still right with the world when the 415 was rolling mainline local No. 7 at speed in the winter of 1949-50 across the Kentucky countryside south of Elizabethtown. The mail and express obviously carried most of the business as the many head end cars attest.

Top: T.W. Dixon, Jr. Collection
Left: W.B. Thurman/T.W. Dixon, Jr. Collection

OTHER ROADS OF THE SOUTH

Winston-Salem Southbound

How many short line railroads could boast of having a standard gauge mallet on their motive power roster during the age of steam? One line that could make this claim was the Winston-Salem Southbound Railway Co.

On June 14, 1941, the "Southbound" acquired a Norfolk and Western Z1b-class 2-6-6-2, No. 1393, and gave it the number, No. 400. The old but still useful Z1b was built by Baldwin in 1914. It had 57" drivers, operated with 225 lbs. of boiler pressure and produced a respectable 75,830 lbs. of tractive effort in compound operation and 90,996 lbs. in simple. Including its tender, No. 400 was over 104 ft., long and nearly 16 ft. high. Speaking of its tender, it carried 26 tons of coal and 18,000 gallons of water. The engine weight of 427,000 pounds gave the 2-6-6-2 good traction when moving heavy tonnage on the up-and-down line between Winston-Salem and Wadesboro N.C.

Called a "Baby Malley" by their crews, No. 400 is shown departing Winston-Salem on June 9, 1949 at 3:00 p.m.—notice the N&W's "banjo" signals to No. 400's right—with 54 cars, heading south toward Wadesboro.

If you did not know better, you would think that we were watching N&W action; however, the number, No. 400, on the Z1b's smokebox and the name, "Winston-Salem Southbound," painted on its tender, would dispel this first impression.

Seeing the old "Z" so far south and away from its parent road was a most enjoyable experience; the 1914 built 2-6-6-2 served the WSSB well for many years.

Ray Carneal/Author's Collection

Shortly after the beginning of the 1900's both the Norfolk and Western and Atlantic Coast line felt that it would be advantageous if a connection between the two roads, other than the one in the Petersburg, Va. area, was built. This additional line would speed up the flow of business between the South and the Mid-west which would, in turn, mean additional revenue for each company. With this in mind, the N&W-ACL began a joint venture to build a line from Winston-Salem, N. C. (Norfolk and Western) to Wadesboro, N. C. (Atlantic Coast Line).

Between 1910-1911 the 92.5 mile line was completed and became known as the Winston-Salem Southbound. Now textile goods, tobacco, agricultural products, etc. from the South could be funneled over this shortcut to the N&W in the "Twin Cities" (Winston-Salem), while coal and finished products, etc. from the North and Mid-West could be sent to Wadesboro and the Atlantic Coast Line. The Winston-Salem Southbound would save both time and mileage, which would mean more income for both the N&W and the ACL. Thus, the WSSB became mainly a bridge route between the two larger roads. Over the following years some on-line business developed on the WSSB. In fact, the road took control of the HPT&D (High Point, Thomasville and Denton) which gave the WSSB access to one of the major furniture manufacturing areas in the United States, especially the "Furniture Capital of the World"-High Point, Thomasville, N. C. and environs.

Soon the WSSB established an acceptable routine which, by 1953, had a daily, nightly through freight-one in each direction-between Winston-Salem and Wadesboro (No. 209 & 212) while a daytime, daily ex-Sunday local freight, in both directions, handled the on-line business (No. 341 & 340) and some through cars as well.

Both the N&W and ACL provided the vast majority of steam motive power for the WSSB, mostly consolidations (2-8-0's), Mikados (2-8-2's) and even an old N&W Z-1b class 2-6-6-2, to handle all traffic until the arrival of the diesels in the 1950's.

An exception to this motive power policy in shown in this photo with one of the daytime locals in the Lexington, N. C. area (Highway U. S. 52 is shown on the right). Mikado No. 300 was built for the WSSB by Baldwin in 1925. Both No. 300 and No. 301, although WSSB engines, were built to the specifications of the M-2 class ACL 2-8-2's: 63" drivers, 200 lbs. of boiler pressure, 59,000 pounds of tractive effort plus an engine weight of 295,150 lbs.

The fireman had a clear stack-this made the company happy although the railfans would have preferred lots of smoke-as the local trundled along with 25 cars in late May of 1949.

The Winston-Salem Southbound still provides some bridge traffic to the now Norfolk Southern Corp. in Winston-Salem and the CSX in Wadesboro. It also remains a most interesting short line with a colorful history.

John Krause/Author's Collection

This is truly a good way to start a railfan's day! Virginian's local passenger train No. 3 is shown ready to leave Norfolk, Va.'s Terminal Station for a trip toward the Blue Ridge Mountains, Roanoke, Va. and Huntington, West Virginia—517.7 miles away. At one time, the VGN's passenger trains made it all the way into Charleston, W. Va. over the rails of the New York Central between Deepwater and Charleston. Unfortunately, all passenger service on the Virginian was discontinued on January 29, 1956.

Mention the Virginian Railroad and one thinks of coal—2-10-10-2's, 2-8-8-2's; coal—2-6-6-4's, 2-8-4's, 2-8-2's and coal. Yet, it operated fine, albeit slow, passenger service, usually pulled by PA-class 4-6-2's. No. 212, heading up today's No. 3 (August 8, 1949) and 3 cars, was built by Richmond in 1920. It had 69" drivers, 200 lbs. of steam pressure and 46,634 pounds of tractive effort plus an engine weight of 298,000 lbs.

It was not long after the Norfolk and Western took control of the Virginian in 1959 that No. 212 was scrapped (January of 1960). Until retired, however, the little PA's provided a most beautiful sight—a 4-6-2 pulling a well run passenger train among all the massive motive power tugging away with those endless coal trains east and hopper trains west.

Both: Ray Carneal/Author's Collection

OTHER ROADS OF THE SOUTH
Virginian Railway

Like so many of the roads depicted in this volume, the Virginian disappeared into a large corporation. These scenes and a lot of the romance of the rails vanished forever with the end of steam and corporate mergers.

H. Reid/T.W. Dixon, Jr. Collection

LEFT

In 1946, the Virginian Railway, which was originally designed to haul coal, coal, coal, purchased 5 new, modern-designed Berkshire-type steam engines from Lima Locomotive Works. They were numbered 505-509 and were used on time freights 71, 72, 73 and 74 between Sewalls Point (Norfolk), Va.-Victoria (crew change point) and Roanoke, Va.

Until the arrival of these BA-class 2-8-4's, Virginian's tonnage was moved by ponderous 2-8-8-2's, monstrous 2-10-10-2's, robust 2-8-2's and powerful electrics. Then, in 1945, the VGN received 8 of the most modern articulated locomotives ever built, their AG-class 2-6-6-6's (No.900-No.907) which were known as the "Blue Ridge" type on the Virginian.

The 2-6-6-6's, which many would, arguably, say were more powerful than Union Pacific's "Big Boys," were complimented with the 5 "berks" which arrived on the property in 1946. Indeed, with the AG's (2-6-6-6's) and BA's (2-8-4's), the Virginian had two of the most modern steamers produced after World War II.

No. 509 had 69" drivers for speed, 69,350 lbs. of tractive effort for pulling power, 460,400 pounds of engine weight for good traction, along with 245 lbs. of boiler pressure.

The BA's proved to be excellent engines and turned in above average performance on VA's time freights and, on occasion, the 2-8-4's also handled themselves quite well hauling coal and hopper trains between Roanoke and the Norfolk area.

Unfortunately these Lima "beauties" only had approximately 10 years of service on the Virginian before being replaced by diesels (made by Fairbanks-Morse) in early 1954. Then, shortly after the December 1959 takeover of the Virginia by the Norfolk & Western, they were scrapped (January of 1960).

I personally saw one of the VGN's 2-8-4's coming into Victoria, Va. (the number escapes me) from the East with a time freight. Even though I was (and remain) a Southern Railway System fan, I was impressed with their sleek looks which, at the same time, exuded the sense of power. It was truly a shame that they were only allowed a decade to put the shine on the rails and revenue in the coffers of the Virginian.

OTHER ROADS OF THE SOUTH

Richmond, Fredericksburg and Potomac

When one thinks of the Pacific type of steam locomotive (4-6-2), a vision of grace, style and speed comes to mind. Richmond, Fredericksburg & Potomac's Pacific No. 303 (shown here) did not meet the normal criteria associated with the greyhound of passenger power. However, this heavy Pacific had a charm of its own with its Elesco feedwater heater and air pumps on the upper side of its smokebox front. Its very bulkiness gave the 4-6-2 a certain look of nonsense, power and efficiency. Indeed, the No. 301-312 series of RF&P's Pacifics were the most popular passenger class of 4-6-2's on the Washington-Richmond line.

No. 303 came from the Richmond Works in 1918. She had 75" drivers, 200 lbs. of steam pressure, an engine weight of 319,000 lbs. and could produce 42,800 pounds of tractive effort; 84 feet long and 15 1/2 feet tall, the 11, 4-6-2's could carry 14 Pullmans north to Washington or 12 passenger cars south to Richmond, Va. (a trip 113 miles long) in approximately 2 1/2 hours (with at least 3 stops in both directions). Of course, with additional cars, its time between the two capitals increased. The tender of No. 303 carried 16 tons of coal and 11,000 gallons of water.

Train No. 79, the *Vacationer*, a winter season schedule, is shown nearing Richmond's beautiful Broad Street station with its all-coach consist this March in 1941. Once at Broad Street, the Atlantic Coast line will take the train-loaded with tourists-on to "sunny" Florida.

The RF&P carried an almost unbelievable volume of traffic, especially passenger runs, on its heavy railed, thick ballasted double track mainline. All the varnish and most of the freights from both the Seaboard Air Line and the Atlantic Coast Line used this speedway between Richmond, Potomac Yard and Washington. Just north of Broad street station was the place to be to watch the parade of trains which, at times, operated with such frequency that it resembled streetcar traffic. During World War II, well over 100 trains per day was a normal occurrence.

Like the Southern Railway System during the era of steam operations, the RF&P had that aesthetical appeal, the style and solemnity of southern railroading which seemed to end north of the Potomac River.

Wiley Bryan/Author's Collection

Approximately one mile south of Alexandria, Va. this Richmond, Fredericksburg & Potomac southbound 8 car troop train gathers speed on its trip to Richmond, Va.-113 miles away. Upfront of this extra was Pacific type 4-6-2 No. 328 on this hot August 14, 1944, afternoon.

Until the arrival of the 600 series 4-8-4's, 328 was one of four 4-6-2's (No. 325-328) which were the most powerful passenger engines on the RF&P and, when in a pinch, they also did quite well when heading a freight run.

With 75" drivers, 225 lbs. of steam pressure, an engine weight of 342,600 lbs. plus 48,266 lbs. of tractive effort, No. 328 could make good time with 16 Pullmans north out of Richmond's Broad Street Station or 14 passenger cars south of Washington's Union Station. At times it was required to hustle 18 cars north and 17 coaches south which it did although at a somewhat slower pace.

Even though not as popular as the No. 301-312 series 4-6-2's, the No. 325-328 group of Pacifics were good performers. Without the impressive Elesco feedwater heater (they had the Worthington 4 1/2 SA heaters) and the air pumps on the smokebox front, it was not considered to be as handsome as the other 4-6-2's; that larger than usual stack also hurt its appearance although they were rather sleek-looking "racers."

No. 328 came from Baldwin in 1927; however, by mid-1947, the RF&P had enough 4-8-4's to cover most of the passenger assignments on the "Capital City Route." At that time, the Chesapeake & Ohio was in need of a heavy passenger Pacific type locomotive for its Louisville-Ashland, Ky. run.   As a result, the C&O purchased No. 325 through No. 328 (328 was renumbered 489) on November 14, 1947, and the ex-RF&P 4-6-2's spent the remaining days of their work on the rails of the C&O.

With the stoker on, No. 328 was shown heading upgrade to pass over the Southern Railway System's double-track, Washington-Atlanta mainline, on its way south to Richmond, Va. This was a good location for rail photographers since all RF&P (Seaboard Air Line-Atlantic Coast Line), Southern and the Chesapeake & Ohio (which used the Southern's mainline from Orange, Va.) trains passed by at speed, in all their glory, at an almost unbelievable number, especially during World War II when over 100 trains per day was nothing unusual!

Those were the days! Thank goodness a few rail photographers visited the area and recorded some of these memorable events so the rest of us could see just how it really was-marvelous!

Richard Cook/Author's Collection

In 1937, the Richmond, Fredericksburg & Potomac purchased its first Northern type of locomotive. They ordered 5 of what became known as the "General" class 4-8-4's (No. 551-555) from the Baldwin Locomotive Works (each engine was named for a Confederate General). They were huge, long, heavy and powerful engines needed for both the extra long Florida passenger runs from the Seaboard Air Line and the Atlantic Coast Line as well as the heavy tonnage freight trains.

Soon after the arrival of the 5 "Generals," the RF&P realized that the No. 551-555 series 4-8-4's were too wide for the First Street Tunnel into Washington's Union Station and too heavy for the bridge-the Long Bridge-over the Potomac River. As a result, the "Generals," which were supposed to be dual purpose, became strictly freight engines which could not venture north of Potomac Yard.

Even though the "Generals" did an outstanding job of moving mile-long freights between Richmond's Acca Yard to Potomac Yard south of Alexandria, Va., the RF&P still needed a big engine to replace their 4-6-2's in order to carry the increasingly long, heavy passenger trips into Washington. As a result of this need, the RF&P turned to Baldwin once more. In 1938, No. 601-606 were delivered to the "Capital Cities Route"- the first of a group of "Governor" class 4-8-4's. The 600's were excellent passenger engines that could handle all the ACL's 4-8-4's and SAL's 4-8-2's could deliver to the RF&P in Richmond (from 18 to 21 heavy steel cars).

The RF&P's "Governor" class dual purpose 4-8-4 locomotives were, arguably, the most handsome Northern type engines to grace the rails. Long, sleek, tastefully painted and lettered, speedy and powerful, the No. 601-612 were named after Virginia governors while No. 613-622 were named after famous Virginians (but they were still called "Governors").

Shown in this dramatic, early morning photo was RF&P's "Governor Benjamin Harrison" (4-8-4 No. 604) leaving Richmond, Va.-near AY tower-at 9:30 a.m., heading north with the pride and joy of the Atlantic Coast Line, No. 88, the *Florida Special*—18 cars (all Pullmans except for the lone baggage car behind No. 604's tender).

No. 604 came from Baldwin in 1938 and had 77" drivers, 260 lbs. of steam pressure, 406,810 lbs. of engine weight and could produce 62,800 lbs. of tractive effort; it was built with a one-piece cast steel locomotive bed frame along with Worthington 5-SA type feedwater heater and a Standard HT stoker. Its Vanderbilt tender held 17 tons of coal and 15,500 gallons of water; the 600's were similar in appearance to the "General" class 4-8-4's; however, they were not as heavy or as wide as the massive 500's.

The aesthetically pleasing and efficient No. 604 was finally retired on March 10, 1953. With this departure, such heart-stirring scenes as shown in this photo vanished forever.

Wiley Bryan/Author's Collection

RIGHT:

One of the most dramatic photos to appear in this book is this time-exposure taken on a cold, windy day in early 1940 at the Richmond, Fredericksburg & Potomac's Acca Yard's engine terminal in Richmond, Va. Not only was this one of the most spectacular pictures, it was also a photo of one of 12 most popular passenger class Pacifics on the RF&P, in this case 4-6-2 No. 307-part of the Elesco feedwater heater equipped No. 301-312 series of 4-6-2's (the tender of Atlantic Coast Line's Pacific No.1612 is shown on the right).

After having its tender filled (16 tons of coal and 11,000 gallons of water) and its engine inspected and washed, No.307, with the air pump heavy smokebox, was now ready for another trip to Washington, D. C.

During their over 30 years of service, these 12 Pacifics handled some of the most famous, popular, "money-making" trains of both the Seaboard Air Line and Atlantic Coast Line on one of the hottest "bridge lines" in the United States. No. 307 finally left the property on April 25, 1950, ending an era of superb steam performance.

Wouldn't it be great to walk among such scenes today, an occasion filled with smoke, steam and those wonderful smells that only the "Iron Horse" could produce?

Bill Griffin Collection

AUTOMATIC
TRAIN CONTROL
SAFETY FIRST ALWAYS

307

Was there ever a more handsome front end of a Northern class 4-8-4?

By the late 1930's, the Florida trains from the Seaboard Air Line and the Atlantic Coast Line, which the Richmond, Fredericksburg and Potomac ferried 113 miles between Richmond, Va. and Washington, D. C., were getting longer and heavier. The RF&P's 300 series 4-6-2's could handle 14 Pullmans north out of Richmond's Broad Street Station without difficulty-in a "pinch" they could even move 15 or 16 cars but at a slower pace; however, trains were running 18 to 21 cars long. The 4-6-2's would have to doublehead to make time with such tonnage or sacrifice speed to get the Pullmans over the "Capital Cities Route." These two alternatives were unacceptable to the RF&P, so a bigger, more powerful locomotive was needed.

The 4-8-4 wheel arrangement seemed to be the answer to the RF&P's problem. As a result, 5 massive and powerful "General" class Northerns (No. 551-555) were delivered to the road from Baldwin in 1937. Unfortunately, the RF&P's Mechanical Department had blundered badly in their planning for these, purportedly, dual-purpose engines, which were named after Confederate generals: they were too heavy for the bridge over the Potomac River (the "Long Bridge") and too large to negotiate the tunnel leading to Washington's Union Station. Due to these errors, the "Generals" became excellent freight engines and served the RF&P with distinction until their retirement on April 17, 1952.

In 1938, the RF&P finally had a big 4-8-4 that could make the trip to Washington with 18 or more cars without difficulty: the 600 series "Governor" class Northerns (No. 601-612 were named after Virginia governors while No.613-622 were given the names of famous Virginians although they were still called "Governors").

No. 602, "Governor Thomas Jefferson," shown at Richmond's Acca (yard) Locomotive Terminal in this excellent time exposure photo made on a windy, cold afternoon in January of 1941, came from Baldwin in 1938. The tractive effort of this quite handsome locomotive was an impressive 62,800 pounds. She was retired on March 10, 1953.

Soon the "Thomas Jefferson" would head a long, heavy varnish north on a trip to Washington and within a few hours it would be back at Broad Street Station with another Florida-bound passenger run for either the SAL or ACL.

These particular days were a railfan's dream come true: steam and steel in action, moving a majority of the nation's people and freight at such a phenomenal rate that it would eventually have a great part to play in our victory over the Axis Powers in World War II.

Bill Griffin Collection

OTHER ROADS OF THE SOUTH

Atlantic Coast Line

Renowned for its relatively gradeless, double-track "speedway" between Richmond, Virginia and Jacksonville, Florida where speeds of 90 m.p.h. and above were commonplace, the Atlantic Coast Line ran some of the most popular and profitable passenger trains on the lucrative New York-Miami route: *Florida Special, Miamian, Vacationer,* (all winter season varnish) plus the *Havana Special, Palmetto Limited, Everglades Limited,* the *Champion,* and others.

For decades the Pacific type 4-6-2 ruled the rails of the "Coast Line" and was the No. 1 form of motive power for its Florida passenger fleet. Most of the ACL's hottest freights were also pulled by the reliable 4-6-2's due to the road's lack of significant grades. However, by the late 1930s the passenger trains were getting longer, heavier and, due to the stiff competition for the Florida business by its neighbor to the west-the Seaboard Air Line (not to mention the Southern Railway System)-speed was becoming an all important factor. The ACL had to make a decision: continue to operate doubleheaded Pacifics to compensate for the new demands placed on its passenger motive power, which was a costly procedure, or purchase heavier and more powerful locomotives.

By this time the SAL, faced with the same problems, had decided on the diesel to pull its streamliners. The ACL, however, remained with steam and selected the popular and proven 4-8-4 Northern type of motive power to solve its dilemma-the famous R-1 class No. 1800-1811. Once on the property, by 1938, the R-1's, due to improper counterbalancing rode rough and did very little to make friends in the track department. Once this error was resolved, however, they put in a performance that made everyone happy: the crews, the track people, passengers and the company.

A prime example of this outstanding ACL motive power is shown in this picture near Richmond's Broad Street Station with 17 cars in March of 1940. No. 1807 was shown at the head of the first of FOUR SECTIONS of the famous *Florida Special,* No. 88, carrying vacationers back north after a stay in sunny and warm Miami. No. 1807 was built at Baldwin in 1938. It had massive 80" drivers, 275 lbs. of steam pressure, an engine weight of 460,270 lbs. and could produce 63,900 lbs. of tractive effort. The 1800-1811 series had cast steel bed frames integral with cylinders, roller bearings on drivers and engine trucks; however, friction bearings were found on all 16 wheels of their huge tender trucks. They possessed HT stokers, Worthington Type SA feedwater heaters and train control. No. 1807 was scrapped on December 31, 1952, spending the last few years in freight service. In fact, it was among the last of the R-1's to leave the ACL's roster after 14 years of service. The Seaboard had the right idea back in the late '30s: the diesel was the future of American railroads.

The photo shows northbound No. 88 heading south! The ACL entered Richmond from the north, headed south to Broad Street Station which had a loop track arrangement. This enabled No. 88 to turn 180° at the station and be pointed north when it was ready to leave Virginia's capital city for Washington behind Richmond, Fredericksburg & Potomac motive power.

Long, large, heavy, powerful, fast with a graphite covered smokebox, white rimmed wheels and a pleasing appearance—these were the ACL's R-1's.

Wiley Bryan/Author's Collection

One might wonder while looking at this photo: "That's a long and heavy passenger train for a Pacific type engine to handle. It must be "a 'plug-run' local." True, it was a lengthy and heavy varnish; however, it was not a local. Instead, it was the Atlantic Coast Line's winter season, plush *Miamian* (No. 72) arriving in Richmond, Virginia's Broad Street Station in March of 1940 at 1:45 p.m. with 4-6-2 No. 1554 pulling the 13 cars of the popular and well patronized, 1st class passenger run.

Until the arrival of the powerful and modern R-1 class 4-8-4's (No. 1800-1811) in 1938, the ACL relied on their Pacifics and Mountain class power (mostly their Pacifics) to move their fleet of Florida varnish. How the 4-6-2's could be so successful can be explained by the fact that the "Coast Line" had a relatively flat and straight Richmond-Jacksonville, double track "fast" mainline.

The Pacifics held their own pulling the Florida fleet until the mid-1930's when the trains grew longer, heavier and speed was becoming an important factor. The ACL had to resort to doubleheading their trains to meet these increasing demands.

Rather than follow the trend of both the Seaboard Air Line and the Southern Railway System who were turning toward the new diesels for motive power, the ACL decided to remain with steam and selected the popular 4-8-4 type Northern, the R-1 class, to meet these increasing demands.

No. 1554 was a product of the Richmond Locomotive Works, class of 1920, and had 73" drivers, 200 lbs. of steam pressure, plus an engine weight of 281,000 lbs. and 40,750 lbs. of tractive effort. It was superheated, had a stoker and was classified as a P-5-A Pacific (No. 1500 through No. 1569). It was also equipped with a "coal pusher" in its tender which helped to keep its coal supply near the stoker screw entry; this device was a great help to the firemen. No. 1554 served the "Coast Line" for 32 years, in both passenger and freight work, being scrapped on Feb. 29, 1952.

No. 72 was pictured entering the labyrinth of tracks and crossovers at the august Broad Street Station which featured a series of "loop" tracks. This explained why this northbound passenger train was actually heading south into the station. When the *Miamian* came to a stop, it would be pointed north once more. After a Richmond, Fredericksburg & Potomac engine replaced No.1554, the heavy varnish would continue its journey north to Washington and, eventually, New York City.

With all the streamliners and locals from both the ACL, SAL and even the Norfolk and Western converging on Broad Street each day, it was a rare moment when things got "quiet" during the steam era. Broad Street Station became a mecca for railfans with the ebb and flow of so many trains-many among the most well-known throughout the country.

Both: Wiley Bryan/Author's Collection

During the steam era, amid all the hot Atlantic Coast Line and Seaboard Air Line Florida fleets of named trains, an occasional local passenger run would pass by. A case in point was ACL's No. 26, shown nearing Richmond, Virginia's Broad Street Station in March of 1942. The local made a daily round trip between Petersburg and Richmond. In fact, the "Coast Line" crews called it the "Petersburg Local." It was the nearest thing the ACL could call a "commuter train."

On this particular day, No. 26 was powered by a light, P-3 class Pacific, No. 438, and had 3 cars in its consist. After a lengthy stay at Broad Street, it would head back to Petersburg, Va.

No. 438, which was originally designed as a dual-purpose engine, i.e., passenger and freight service, came from Baldwin in 1915. This light, tall stacked "dowager" had 69" drivers, 226,800 lbs. of engineer weight plus 200 lbs. of steam pressure. She had 33,400 lbs. of tractive effort and was superheated. In August of 1951, the ACL renumbered her No. 2438; then, on November 4, 1951-only 3 months later-the scrap dealers had another victim of "progress." To the right of No. 438 was the Seaboard Air Line's Hermitage Yard.

The ACL local was pictured on the tracks of the Richmond, Fredericksburg & Potomac which took all ACL and SAL passenger and freight trains north to Potomac Yard and/or Washington, D.C.'s Union Station.

This was the location in Richmond (between Broad Street Station and "AY" Tower)-where the ACL's mainliners from Jacksonville, Florida joined the RF&P-the railfans congregated to watch the ebb and flow of the tremendous volume of trains. During World War II, you rarely experienced a moment when a train was not in sight. It remains a good spot; however, watch out for the rail police for they will consider you a trespasser.

This scene is a prime example of railroading in a time when people used trains to travel and before the diesel removed steam from the rails forever.

It's late afternoon in Richmond, Virginia, near Broad Street Station, in March of 1940, as the Atlantic Coast Line's *Vacationer*-No. 79 (a winter season passenger run)-heads north in order to head south to Florida!

The Richmond, Fredericksburg & Potomac brought No. 79 to Richmond from Washington, D. C., used the "loop track" at Broad Street so when it came to a stop at the station, it was heading north. While at rest, this massive and yet sleek ACL 4-8-4, No. 1803-an R-1 class Northern-replaced the RF&P's motive power.

Since the "Coast Line" entered Richmond from the North, No. 79 would leave Virginia's capital city heading north; at "AY" tower (less than a

mile north of the station) the big 4-8-4 would cross over all RF&P tracks and then head south on home rails. By morning, this popular winter varnish would be in the "Sunshine State." To the left of No. 1803, you can see part of the Seaboard Air Line's Hermitage yard.

No. 1803 came from Baldwin in 1938, and was one of 12 huge R-1 class 4-8-4's (No. 1800-1811) to take on the SAL. All that power and yet it looked clean with graphite on the front of its smokebox. Modern in every way, the R-1's had roller bearings on the engine drivers and trucks (friction bearings were used on the tender trucks, however); a standard HT stoker and Worthington type SA feedwater heater helped to improve its efficiency and the Northern had a cast steel bed frame integral with cylinders and train control.

The R-1's, after a counterbalance problem was resolved, remained the major passenger power on the ACL until the late 1940's when purple and silver colored diesels appeared on the property. Once the diesels got their foot in the "Coast Line's" door, No. 1803 and her sisters were relegated to freight assignments where they performed with great elan until they were scrapped (No. 1803 met its demise on December 20, 1951).

Be that as it may, on this chilly March afternoon in 1940, the R-1's were THE locomotive on the ACL's hot Richmond-Jacksonville double track mainline and could really "pick 'em up and lay 'em down."

All seemed so right in the rail world this particular day.

Wiley Bryan/Author's Collection

Rocky Mount, N. C. was and still remains a great train-watching location since the mainline of the Atlantic Coast Line Railroad (now CSX) splits the town in half. In fact, the double track main separates two North Carolina counties—Nash and Edgecombe—as well.

On September 11, 1947, local passenger No. 48 was found at Rocky Mount's station taking on mail, express, some L-C-L and passengers. No. 48 ran from Wilmington, N. C. to Portsmouth, Va.

Today, the local is powered by one of the ACL's P-5-B class 4-6-2's No. 1635 which had 69" drivers; its engine weight was 281,685 pounds and had 45,275 lbs. of tractive effort. They also had a good stoker and a coal pusher in its tender.

The P-5-B's were originally built by Baldwin between 1922 and 1926 as a dual-purpose Pacific which, for many years, was the standard mainline freight locomotive of the "Coast Line." Later it was found that they were also capable of making good time with heavy passenger trains as well. Eventually 165 P-5-B's were built. They stood nearly 15' high and were over 80' long from the cowcatcher to the tender coupler.

No. 1635 came from Baldwin in 1923 and was retired on January 31, 1952—nearly 3 decades of service for the ACL (notice the ACL's symbol on the side of the clean tender).

Like most southern motive power during the age of steam operations, the "Coast Line's" P-5-B's were aesthetically pleasing to the eye and very dependable. Indeed, No. 1635 simply looked good!

Ray Carneal/Author's Collection

The Chesapeake & Ohio was renowned for its photogenic and yet powerful and efficient steam motive power. The F-18 class 4-6-2, No. 482-shown here at Hampton, Va. on February 22, 1946 (a Friday morning)-was no exception to the road's reputation for handsome locomotives.

To call No. 482 "just another Pacific type engine" would not do justice to the big 4-6-2. Indeed, it would be an understatement of monumental proportions. Look at her: the smokebox front was almost completely covered with air pumps and other accouterments, its engine weighed 334,420 lbs., the boiler pressure was set for 200 pounds while its tractive effort was a most impressive 46,900 lbs. (The cylinder horsepower was 2,624); No. 482 had 74" drivers and its huge tender (347,000 lbs.-28 tons of coal and 18,000 gallons of water) made the F-18's among the largest, most powerful Pacific type locomotive ever built and it had a boiler big enough to sustain its power. Yet, with all this "muscle," No. 482 was a good looking engine!

The Richmond Locomotive Works delivered six very large 4-6-2's (classed as F-18's) to the C&O in June and July of 1923 to help the F-17 class Pacifics which, for almost a decade, had been the mainstay of the 4-6-2 fleet (No. 482 was placed on the roster in June of that year). These new engines were originally numbered No. 188-193; however, in 1924, they were renumbered No. 480-485.

No. 482, photographed here pulling No. 42, *The George Washington,* spent a great deal of its life on the C&O's Washington Subdivision, going to and from Washington, D. C., heading to the nation's capital over the Southern Railway System's mainline north of Charlottesville, Va.

The F-18's did an outstanding job for the C&O until the arrival of the diesels. This famous class of motive power was retired in December of 1952-a sad time for the steam gods and railfans.

Compact, powerful and fast, the F-18's justly deserved their honored niche in the history of the Chesapeake & Ohio, for they were a marvel to behold while pulling varnish along the "Chessie" during those unforgettable years when steam ruled the rails.

Richard Cook/Author's Collection

Other Roads Of The South

Chesapeake & Ohio

They were affectionately called "Big Mikes" (Mikados) by their crews and the Chesapeake & Ohio's K-4 class 2-8-4's proved to be one of the most versatile and admired locomotives on the road's roster. Why? The 2700's had all the modern devices available at the time of their birth. The K-4's could lug coal drags, hotshot merchandise and even heavy varnish; they rode like Pullmans and were mostly trouble-free in operation—the 2-8-4's could do it all and in a most efficient and impressive manner.

A good example of the 2-8-4 which, on the C&O, were called "Kanawhas" rather than the usual "Berkshire" for this wheel arrangement (named after the river which they followed for so many miles in the heart of the mountains), was shown approaching Handley, West Virginia on June 6, 1956 (a Wednesday) at 10:40 a.m. with a 52-car freight (called the "Bulldog" by the crews in this area) from Russell, Kentucky. No. 2770, a 1947 "graduate" from ALCO, had 69" drivers, an engine weight of 469,680 lbs. and a boiler pressure of 245 lbs. It had a cast steel bed frame with integral cylinders plus roller bearings on all axles along with a Standard HT stoker; No. 2770 could produce a total of 83,350 lbs. of tractive effort (including a booster which made an additional 14,000 lbs. available). The tender of this large and powerful "Big Mike" weighed 394,100 lbs. and held 30 tons of coal plus 21,000 gallons of water—both engine and tender stretched to a length of 105 feet. Even though you could find these Kanawhas on most of the C&O, they were seen most frequently on runs over the Clifton Forge-Richmond-Newport News, Va. mainline.

The first batch (No. 2700-2739) came from the American

Locomotive Company (ALCO); No. 2740-2749 arrived from Lima in 1945; Lima also built No. 2750-2759 in early 1947 and ALCO delivered the last group (No. 2760-2789) in late 1947. These statistics will give you undeniable evidence in the faith placed in the 2-8-4's by the C&O. By mid-1952, however, GM's F-7's began replacing these smooth riding and dependable locomotives which, like most of the steamers on the C&O, had an aesthetically pleasing, compact appearance. The last of these remarkable K-4 class 2-8-4's were scrapped in May of 1961.

One item concerning this photo: it looks somewhat "grainy." This was not due to the camera's quality. Instead, the less than sharp effect was due to the "3 H's" which could be found south of the Mason-Dixon line during the summer months: heat, humidity and haze! By the way, the Kanawha River was just out of the photo to the right.

LEFT:

Coal—For most of its existence it was the "No.1" source of revenue for the Chesapeake & Ohio. Even today, the "black stuff" plays a major roll in filling the coffers of the CSX.

Looking at a map of the C&O during the 1920-1950's period, one would find what appeared to be a series of "spider webs" stretching over the states of West Virginia, Kentucky and western Virginia—all lines engineered to reach the coal mines. Most of these "webs" had sharp curves, stiff grades, tunnels, bridges and many were almost inaccessible to the outside world except by rail.

After trying several forms of motive power to get the coal out of these isolated locations, the so-called "boondocks," in the heart of the mountains, the Chesapeake & Ohio decided that the 2-6-6-2 compound Mallet was the most effective locomotive design to get the job done during the steam era. Indeed, their H-1 and H-2 class 2-6-6-2's performance convinced the road that this class of Mallet compound was THE engine for its mountain regions.

Once on the property (1910) the 2-6-6-2's even did an admirable job handling mainline runs and remained in this service until replaced by more modern, powerful, more efficient and faster engines such as the 2-8-8-2's, 2-10-4's as well as the unique and magnificent 2-6-6-6's. In fact, as newer power appeared, the 2-6-6-2's found themselves relegated to the less glamorous but essential mine runs over these mountain "webs" plus in yards putting together the tremendous tonnage trains for mainline runs.

A good example of these dirty and strenuous assignments is shown here as two H-4 class 2-6-6-2's struggle to get its 21 cars of coal, near Logan, West Virginia, on towards the big mainline yard at Huntington, West Virginia. The grades in this area were so severe that this was actually the first half of Extra 1468 north as the coal train was shown "doubling the hill" on May 19, 1955 at 12:18 p.m. Imagine, two powerful 2-6-6-2's limited to only 21 cars! Some grade!

Both H-4's pictured here on a Thursday came from the Richmond Works (No.1468 in 1918 and No.1331 in 1912). This successful class of 2-6-6-2's had an engine weight of 435,000 lbs. while the tender (Vanderbilt style) topped the scales at 219,100 lbs. (15 tons of coal and 12,000 gallons of water); the boiler pressure was 200 lbs. and they had a tractive effort of 74,200 lbs. in compound and 93,600 lbs. in simple operations. Both No. 1468 and No. 1331 had 56" drivers and were 105'11" in total length. There were eventually 150 H-4's on the C&O's roster.

Both: Bob Malinoski/Author's Collection

Chesapeake & Ohio's mighty H-8 class 2-6-6-6 Allegheny No. 1624, all 1,197,400 lbs. of her, is shown with through freight No. 99 in the Handley, West Virginia area, (running between Hinton, West Virginia and Russell, Kentucky) on June 6, 1956-a Wednesday-at 3:57 p.m. The H-8 was using all of its 110,200 lbs. of tractive effort (4,734 cylinder horsepower), blasting its way west, literally shaking the ground-and the photographer-to get its 64 cars towards its destination.

It was hard to fathom just how large and brutishly powerful this example of what the Lima Locomotive Works (its maker) called "Super Power" really was. This photo does not do justice to the immensity of this locomotive with twin-stacks and a 6-wheel trailer truck. You simply had to be there to truly understand why many locomotive connoisseurs considered the Allegheny to be the world's largest and most powerful steam locomotive ever built.

Lima, which constructed sixty of the Alleghenies for the C&O and eight for the Virginian (which called them "Blue Ridges" and classified them as "AG's"—No. 900-907), was so impressed with their efforts that they used the 2-6-6-6's in most of their advertisements for several years.

Needless to say, the Chesapeake & Ohio was thoroughly impressed with the performance of their H-8's. Indeed, they received the 2-6-6-6's as fast as Lima could make them: No. 1600-1609 (Dec. 1941-Jan. 1942), No. 1610-1619 (Sept. 1942-Oct. 1942), No. 1620-1629 (July 1944-Aug. 1944), No. 1630-1644 (Oct. 1944-Dec. 1944) and No. 1645-1659 (Oct. 1948-Dec. 1948). The Virginian received their 8 AG's in 1945.

Everything about the Allegheny was massive, including their tender: 260 lbs. of boiler pressure, 67" drivers, 125'8" long and nearly 16 feet tall plus over 80,000 lbs. of weight on each set of drivers. The tender held 25 tons of coal and 25,000 gallons of water and was so heavy it had a 3-axle Buckeye truck upfront followed by a unique 4-axle truck on the rear.

On one occasion, while running on the Russell to Walbridge, Ohio line, an H-8 developed a maximum drawbar horsepower of 7,498 in moving a 14,083 ton coal train (160 cars) at almost 30 m.p.h.-fantastic!

In late 1956, however, it was all over, for the C&O finally achieved complete dieselization by this time. We are fortunate that two of the C&O's magnificent 2-6-6-6's escaped the scrapper's torch and were preserved (No. 1601 and 1604).

Their thunderous exhaust can still be remembered by many who saw them in action, battling the area from which their name was derived: The Alleghenies. Lima was good! Real good!

Sounding like an approaching thunderstorm and feeling like an earthquake, Chesapeake & Ohio's mightiest of the steam giants on its roster, the massive, million pounder H-8 class 2-6-6-6 Allegheny, No. 1644, is shown on an extra westbound mixed freight blasting into Handley, West Virginia on a run from Hinton, W. Va. with 125 cars at 4:45 p.m., July 6, 1956 (a Wednesday).

Truly, this is a photo of what became known as one of the finest examples of a "SuperPower" locomotive: every modern appliance available was placed on this engine and its sister H-8's to enable it to pull more tonnage at a greater speed with less maintenance and to do it all at less cost to the company as compared to the motive power that preceded it.

The simple articulated H-8's were an instant success on the C&O, even out performing the slower but powerful H-7 class 2-8-8-2's. Between December 1941 and December 1948, Lima Locomotive Works delivered 60 of the 2-6-6-6's (No. 1600-1659) to the C&O. No. 1644 joined their roster in December of 1944. Lima also built eight of these "bruisers" for the Virginian (No. 900-907) in 1945.

During their reign, the Alleghenies could be found over a goodly portion of the Chesapeake & Ohio, especially from Russell, Kentucky to even Newport News, Virginia as well as the line from Russell to Walbridge, Ohio where they helped another "SuperPower" locomotive move the tonnage, C&O's massive and impressive T-1 class 2-10-4's (No. 3000-3039) that weighed a hefty 981,000 lbs. and could produce 93,350 lbs. of tractive effort.

How could so much power and weight be placed into such a compact, aesthetically pleasing-just plain good looking-locomotive? Lima and the C&O did their work well to contain this much energy into a package that amazed the railroad world and all who saw them in action.

Both: Bob Malinoski/Author's Collection

A 2-6-6-6: The wheel arrangement was almost unimaginable, yet exciting; the locomotive that used those wheels and drivers was monstrous in size yet beautiful, powerful but easy to handle, weighed over one million pounds yet could move tonnage at 60 m.p.h., bigger in many respects than Union Pacific's "Big Boy" (4-8-8-4), yet it was compact, aesthetically pleasing to the eye and, arguably, the world's largest and most powerful steam locomotive ever built and truly the best ever produced by the "cadillac" of locomotive builders - Lima (an ideal example of what Lima called "Super Power!").

Shown here is No. 1627 pulling a westbound hopper train of 160 cars-with east-at Kanawha Falls, West Virginia (running between Hinton and Handley, West Virginia) on June 16, 1956-a Wednesday-at 1:33 p.m. Just look at its awesome statistics: 67" drivers, 260 lbs. of boiler pressure, an engine weight of 771,300 lbs. plus a 426,100 lb. tender equaled a total of 1,197,400 pounds (over 80,000 lbs. on each pair of drivers); a tractive effort of 110,200 lbs. and a cylinder horsepower of 4,734. No. 1627 stretched to a length of 125'8" and its tender, which held 25 tons of coal and 25,000 gallons of water, was equipped with Buckeye six and eight-wheel flexible-frame trucks; the 2-6-6-6 had a cast steel engine bed with integral cylinders, Timken roller bearings on all driving axles along with the Standard MB stoker.

The first of the sixty H-8 class 2-6-6-6's, which the Chesapeake & Ohio named "Alleghenies," arrived on the property December 10, 1941, and the road was immediately sold on these million-pound giants. Not only was the C&O impressed by these huge engines, Lima was so proud of their product that they used the 2-6-6-6 in their brochures and other advertisements for many years. The Virginian Railroad was the only other road to order 2-6-6-6's, receiving 8 of them (No. 900-907) in 1945. Indeed, Lima, C&O and the Virginian had good reasons to be proud of these magnificent locomotives!

Their main operating territory covered the areas from Russell, Kentucky to Clifton Forge, Va. as well as Russell to Walbridge, Ohio. On occasion, they were even found in Newport News, Va. By the mid-1950's, however, diesels had replaced these Lima beauties. Fortunately, two of these Alleghenies (No. 1601 and 1604) were preserved by the C&O.

They were truly poetry and power in motion!

Bob Malinoski/Author's Collection

STEAM RETURNS
The Excursion Era

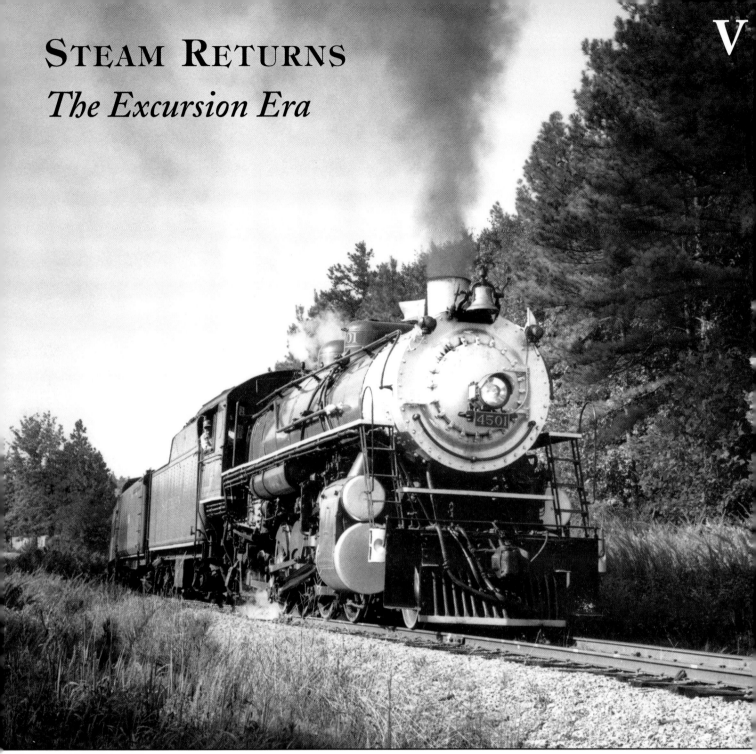

U sing every ounce of its 53,900 lbs. of tractive effort and a great deal of sanding, No. 4501 fights it way upgrade near Butner, N. C. on an East Durham, N. C. to Keysville, Va. roundtrip excursion with 15 heavy cars this August 6, 1977, at 8:40 a.m. The roar from its stack was tremendous!

This Southern Railway System Ms class (M=Mikado, S=Superheated) 2-8-2 had polished the rails of the road that "Served the South" for 38 years; it was a product of the Baldwin Locomotive Works (class of 1911).

After working 16 years for the Kentucky & Tennessee, which purchased No. 4501 from the Southern on October 7, 1948 for $8,225 (K&T renumbered the Southern's first 2-8-2 to No. 12), it was purchased by Paul H. Merriman for $5,000 in 1964 and placed in excursion service that same year with its original number restored. By 1966, it was painted green and gold along with a great deal of white trimming and, as they say, the rest was history.

It was 96° F and very humid this August 6th as No. 4501 headed to Keysville. I followed the famous 2-8-2 all the way from Durham to Keysville and back to Durham. It was 11 hours, 173 miles of a great adventure, one I will never forget. Indeed, I did not have a dry stitch of clothing on me that late afternoon and I slept well that night. More than likely, I had a smile on my face the entire night since I had experienced an event that would stay with me for the remainder of my life.

It is still hard to fathom the love this old 1911 build Mikado engendered among the thousands of people who rode her, photographed her and watched her. The Southern's first of nearly 400 2-8-2's left her mark in rail history. In fact No. 4501 still sees action from time to time to this very day-89 years after Baldwin built her!

Curt Tillotson, Jr.

The *Carolina Special* (actually Extra 722 South)—Keysville, Va.-August 23, 1980-1:30 p.m.-86° F (sunny)-Southern Railway System's Ks-1 class Consolidation (2-8-0) No. 722-8 cars—on a Richmond-Keysville (Va.)-East Durham-Raleigh (N. C.) steam excursion-rather than "a face only a mother could love," we have a "face EVERYONE could love." Beautiful!

Curt Tillotson, Jr.

The 4501 was still a distant memory as Kentucky and Tennessee No. 12 is working loaded coal just a mile west of Stearns, Kentucky on this splendid September 3, 1963. The temperature is hot this day, but the fall is rapidly approaching, and with it the end of steam on the K&T.

Fortunately for thousands of railfans, Paul Merriman of Chattanooga, Tennessee had the foresight to purchase the little Mikado from the K&T after the diesels arrived and took the ex-Southern locomotive to Chattanooga that made the Southern's steam program a success!

Elmer Trealor/T.W. Dixon, Jr. Collection

I got lucky! Just minutes before this Raleigh, N. C.-bound steam excursion passed before my camera lens, it was cloudy and "gloomy." Then, just seconds before Extra 722 South crossed over former Highway U. S. 15, now part of Geer Street in the Gorman, N. C. area, the sun broke out in brilliant fashion and remained so just long enough to highlight one of the most handsome Consolidations I've ever seen. By the time its last passenger car passed by, the thick clouds returned. Yes, I, and now the readers of this book, got lucky!

The Southern Railway System ran Extra 722 South from Richmond, Va. to Raleigh on August 23, 1980. My photo of the majestic-looking 2-8-0, No. 722, was made at 5:30 p.m. with the temperature standing at a humid 86° F.

No. 722 was born at the Baldwin Locomotive Works in 1904. The Southern eventually classified the Consolidation as a Ks-1 which had 56" drivers, carried 200 lbs. of steam pressure; its engine weighed nearly 214,000 lbs. And it produced nearly 44,000 pounds of tractive effort. She worked for the Southern until the early 1950's and, fortunately, No. 722 and sister 2-8-0 No. 630 were sold to the East Tennessee & Western North Carolina, thereby escaping the scrapper's torch.

Due to the popularity of its growing excursion program, the Southern needed to augment its steam power and remove some of the burdens from the extremely successful 2-8-2 No. 4501. As a result, the Southern contacted the East Tennessee & Western North Carolina and agreed to swap two of their diesels for steamers No. 722 (which was numbered 208 while with the ET&WNC) and No. 630, painted them green and gold to have them ready for the 1969-70 excursion service; the two 2-8-0's were put into excellent condition. Indeed, the care given to the two Consolidations would rival the maintenance crew's efforts of the 1920's and 1930's.

By 1980, No. 722 was immensely popular and it was used mostly in branch line work while the larger excursion engines were confined to "big rail" territory, i.e. mainline service.

This particular day No. 722 was needed in the Raleigh area in order to cover several runs in eastern North Carolina. As a result, the Southern called the extra south as the *Carolina Special* and ran it, along with its 8 cars, from Richmond to Keysville, Va. (where it took on coal and water), then down the Keysville-East Durham, N. C. line and finally on to Raleigh, N. C. over the Southern's Greensboro-Goldsboro route.

I followed No. 722 from Burkeville, Va. to East Durham. Clouds plagued me off and on during my "adventure;" however, this particular moment, just a few miles north of East Durham, with the sun accentuating the lines of this beautiful 2-8-0, my journey seemed to be worthwhile.

Isn't it a thing to admire? No. 722 was truly poetry in motion! It's true: a picture is worth a thousand words!

Both: Curt Tillotson, Jr.

By 1980, the Southern was looking for a more powerful steam locomotive to help pull longer excursion trains at a faster pace. After inspecting ex-C&O's No. 2716, the Southern signed a 5-year lease with the Kentucky Railway Museum for the service of No. 2716 and moved the 2-8-4 to its Birmingham, Alabama Steam Shops in order to have the K-4 ready for the 1982 excursion season.

No. 2716's handsome appearance was not the only thing that attracted her to the Southern, for its vital statistics were equally impressive: a tractive effort of 66,450 lbs. plus an additional 14,400 lbs. from its booster; 245 lbs. of steam pressure, an engine weight of 460,000 pounds, which gave it good adhesion when pulling tonnage, and a tender (30 tons of coal plus 26,000 gallons of water) that topped the scales at 390,000 lbs. and the K-4 was slightly over 105 feet long from engine to tender.

It's 10:00 a.m. on July 4, 1982, with the temperature near 88° F, as we see Extra 2716 North approaching Danville, Va. on a Greensboro, N. C.-Alexandria, Va. excursion with 17 cars.

Even though its time on the Southern was short, it was most memorable. The Kanawha was truly a most attractive, compact, well-designed and a good performer; the 2-8-4 was very popular with the fans (including your author). Imagine seeing a 2-8-4 painted green and gold pulling the *Crescent*—FANTASTIC!

This was how I spent my 4th of July in 1982: following ex-Chesapeake & Ohio's K-4 class 2-8-4 No. 2716 from Reidsville, N. C. to Monroe, Va. on the Southern Railway System's Washington-Atlanta mainline. It was a decision I never regretted. In fact, it was one of the most truly enjoyable Fourths I've ever experienced.

In 1980, the Southern signed a 5-year lease with the Kentucky Railway Museum so it could use this handsome ex-C&O Kanawha, built by the American Locomotive Works in 1943 for duel service (freight and passenger).

No. 2716 served the C&O from 1943 through 1956 (put out to pasture by the diesels). Then, in 1959, she was placed on display in Louisville, Ky. under the care of the Kentucky Railway Museum.

After securing the services of this powerful engine (69,350 lbs. of tractive effort with an additional 14,400 pounds from its booster) the Southern crews in the steam excursion shops in Birmingham, Alabama went to work. On October 8, 1981, fire returned to its massive boiler. Two days later the 2-8-4 went on a shakedown roundtrip from Birmingham to Chattanooga, Tennessee with freight tonnage tied on to its huge tender. As a result of this October 10th trip, No. 2716 was pronounced ready for the 1982 excursion season. Unfortunately, it was not able to complete the season due to serious problems in No. 2716's firebox. The ailment was so bad the Southern had to rent NKP's 2-8-4 No. 765 to complete the 1982 assignments; soon No. 2716 was returned to the Kentucky Railway Museum.

This July 4, 1982, No. 2716 headed Extra 2716 North on a Greensboro, N. C. to Alexandria, Va. excursion with 17 cars. I photographed this scene in historic Monroe, Virginia where it was refueled and watered at 3:00 p.m. on a cloudy day with the temperature near 88° F.

The American flags placed near the extra's white flags was a nice touch since it was Independence Day. The Southern symbol on the front shields and the brass eagle over the headlight (which had been moved up from the cowcatcher area-a C&O practice-to a slightly below center position on its graphite covered smokebox) really added to its already good looks. These "extra touches" really "Southernized" the K-4. Indeed, many aficionados of Southern steam power felt that it represented what a Southern owned 2-8-4 might have looked like if the road had purchased modern steam power rather than turning to the diesel for its future motive power.

The high-sided "gon" to the left of No. 2716 held the coal for the steamer while many of the fans watched this anachronism and marveled at its appearance, its smells, its sounds. They were experiencing why the steam locomotive was the most human-like machine ever produced by man.

Within 10 minutes the 460,000 pounds of engine and 390,000 lbs of tender, which held 30 tons of coal and 21,000 gallons of water, will come alive with that magnificent steamboat whistle wide open, headed towards Alexandria.

Yes, it was one of the most memorable 4th of July that I can remember!

Curt Tillotson, Jr.

Extra 1 North is shown sitting in Spartanburg, S. C. on September 5, 1976, at 8:18 a.m., ready to head north to Elkhorn City, Kentucky, 277 miles away, on the Clinchfield Railroad, pulling what was known as the "Autumn Leaf Special"-a very popular excursion during the mid to late 1970's.

The little, but spry 4-6-0 will need the help of the two, 1,500 h.p. F-7B's hooked on behind (No. 250 and No. 869) to complete its journey on one of the most rugged and scenic lines east of the Mississippi River.

This is truly a photo of an anachronism still in service! This clean 4-6-0 was built in April of 1882 in the Logansport (Indiana) Shops of the Columbus, Chicago and Indianapolis Central Railroad and number 423. After serving on several short lines under different numbers, No. 1 wound up on the Clinchfield in the early 1900's and it was then leased to the Black Mountain Railroad. On December 7, 1955, it was sold to the town of Erwin, Tennessee for display. In 1968, the Clinchfield Management decided to use the 4-6-0 for excursion service. Soon it became obvious the "10-wheeler" would need help with the grades, sharp curves, tunnels and other adverse conditions presented by the Appalachian Mountain Range. After all, No. 1 could only muster 15,100 lbs. of tractive effort, had 125 pounds of boiler pressure; stood 13 ft. high and was 57 ft.-6 inches long from engine to tender (it held 8 1/2 tons of coal and only 2,960 gallons of water).

Its first trip was made on November 23, 1968. Soon, two F-7B's were added for the extra power: No. 250, which had a steam generator, and No. 869, which was equipped with a steam line; one of the "growlers" even carried an additional 2,150 gallons of water for No. 1.

The "One Spot" was a big success. It traveled up and down the Clinchfield, all over the Seaboard Coast Line (down to Tampa, Florida, over to Raleigh, N. C. and so on), the Piedmont & Northern-even on the Southern Railway System.

Unfortunately, on June 10, 1979, No. 1 suffered a broken frame near the journal box on the rear driver. Try as they may, the Clinchfield maintenance crews could not repair it to a condition that would meet the safety codes for excursion service. Finally it was placed in the Baltimore & Ohio Railroad Museum. Then, after much work, No. 1 was steamed-up and chugged around the museum area on June 18, 1983. She can be seen at the museum this very day.

Imagine: built in 1882 and still in action in 1983! The "Little Guy" won the hearts of thousands of fans who will never forget the "One Spot!" By the way, rumor has it that the 4-6-0 powered the first relief train into Johnstown, Pa. after the Great Flood of 1889! Fact or fiction?

Both: Curt Tillotson, Jr.

Who would have thought that one day a Canadian Pacific Royal Hudson steam locomotive would grace the rails of the Southern Railway System? Believe it or not, on July 14, 1979, at 10:05 a.m., with the temperature hovering near an uncomfortable 90° F, this fantasy became a reality.

From this photo we see a Canadian Pacific H-1-c class 4-6-4 Royal Hudson powering a 12-car Alexandria, Va.-bound excursion nearing Danville, Va. on the Southern's Washington-Atlanta mainline at nearly 45 m.p.h.

Built by the Montreal Locomotive Works in 1937, this 4-6-4, No. 2839, had 75" drivers-the tallest drivers of all the steam engines ever operated in excursion service on the Southern-with a tractive effort of 45,300 pounds plus a booster which produced an additional 12,000 lbs. of T.E. It's engine and tender weighed nearly 659,500 lbs. For excursion purposes, No. 2839 was assigned an ex-Louisville & Nashville tender which made an extra 20,000 gallons of water available for the thirsty semi-streamlined Royal Hudson.

The No. 2839's last regular service for its parent road was in 1959; however, it was saved from the scrapper's torch and, in 1979, the Southern signed a 2-year lease for this high stepping lady. As a result, between 1979 and 1980-81, the South got a good look at this "stranger" from Canada. Other than the name, "Southern Railway System," there was one additional feature added to No. 2839 to make the 4-6-4 more "Southernized:" a steamboat whistle off Southern's Ps-4 No. 1406 gave it a sound so familiar to those of us who remember the Southern when steam ruled the rails.

This is probably one of the most dramatic photographs that I made during the steam excursion era.

Here is the situation that brought about this wonderful encounter: It's March 22, 1981; the Seaboard Coast Line (part of the Family Line's System) hosted the "Family Line's Safety Express"-running as 2nd No. 82 (Amtrak's No. 82, the "Silver Star," passed through the area earlier in the day)-which was powered by a June 1948 Lima built 4-8-4, No. 614 (an ex-Chesapeake & Ohio J-3a class Greenbrier-the C&O would NEVER call a 4-8-4 "Northern").

No. 614 had 22 cars with several hundred passengers on board this cold (38° F), cloudy day, as it approached a landmark on the old Seaboard Air Line's Virginia Division (part of their Richmond-Miami mainline): the deep-cut at Bracey, Virginia which the SAL crews nicknamed the "Grand Canyon of the East."

I followed 2nd No. 82 from Raleigh, N. C. to Bracey. I knew I had to get a photo of this handsome J-3a working through "Bracey Cut." I got lucky! An SCL trainmaster was standing on the overpass, along with approximately 15 railfans including yours truly, as No. 614 approached. He took his portable radio and called No. 614: "614-we've got a large group of fans on the Bracey overpass. Let's give them a great show!" Looking at the photo, you can see that No. 614's crew complied with this kindhearted trainmaster's request.

Just look at this magnificent scene. The stocker, booster, cylinder cocks, safety valve-everything-were all opened and a great plume of smoke was shooting skyward out of that massive stack as the engineer yanked down on the whistle cord. I could not breath; I just stared, slack-jawed, my eyes were as big as 50¢ pieces. In fact, I am surprised that I still had enough control of myself to release the camera shutter in order to record this moment in time.

The struggling 4-8-4 had 74" drivers and a tractive effort of 66,450 lbs. plus an extra 12,400 lbs. from its booster. The engine weighed 482,200 pounds while its tender, which carried 25 tons of coal and 21,500 gallons of water, topped the scale at 386,130 lbs. She worked for the C&O from 1948 until 1956. Then Ross Rowland bought No. 614 and ran the J-3a on its first excursion in July of 1982; it is still in operational condition to this very day.

Steam and steel, battling upgrade, the whistle wide open, moving at 15 m.p.h. with 22 cars-it was a piece of rail history that I recorded on film. Hopefully, the reader, when looking at this picture, will be able to sense my excitement, my enjoyment of such action that will not be witnessed again, at least not in this area. The CSX took up the track through Bracey in 1987. What a great loss but, still, what a great picture!

Both: Curt Tillotson, Jr.

A portrait of "Modern Steam Power at Rest." There's 84,600 pounds of tractive effort and 448,000 lbs. of locomotive behind that massive, brutish and yet aesthetically pleasing, magnificent face of Texas & Pacific's 2-10-4, I-1a class heavy mauler, No. 610.

In between excursion assignments, we find the oil-burner in Greensboro, N. C. on July 12, 1978 at 8:45 a.m. Just 4 days later (July 16th) the "monster" will be alive, spouting smoke and steam on a trip to Alexandria, Va. with 20 cars of fans-all who would experience an adventure they would long remember.

No. 610 came from the erection shops of Lima in 1927-one of 70 Texas-types owned by the Texas & Pacific-and leased to the Southern Railway System in 1977. It had 63" drivers, 109 ft. long (including its tender); stood almost 16 ft. high with a boiler pressure of 255 lbs. and cost the T&P $107,120—what a bargain!

By 1981, the Texas-type engine was back home in Fort Worth, Texas. She might have departed the rails of the Southern but the memory of those flashing rods, oil smoke shooting skyward, the low moan of her steamboat whistle, that huge Elesco feedwater heater and much, much more remains in the hearts of those who saw No. 610 in action. Now, through photos such as this one, those who were not at trackside watching the I-1a class 2-10-4 roll by, leaving soot on their hands and face, will get a sense of what it was like, the joy and excitement that the oil-burner produced.

After a long run on its maiden voyage from Birmingham, Alabama to Lynchburg, Va., No. 611 accumulated some road grime on its streamlined shroud. With the news media waiting for its arrival at the place of its birth, Roanoke, Va., the Norfolk Southern Corp. decided to wash the big Northern so it would look its best in front of the cameras when it finished this historic pilgrimage.

After leaving the ex-Southern Railway System's Washington-Atlanta mainline just south of Lynchburg's Montview Yard, Extra 611 North traveled over a connection track to the ex-Norfolk and Western's Kenny Yard and the mainline to Roanoke and points west. Now, Extra 611 West is shown this August 22, 1982 at 12:05 p.m. being groomed for the many people waiting in Roanoke. I counted 14 giant-size boxes of Tide washing powder that were used to wash the J-class 4-8-4, making it clean enough "to eat off of."

In the crowd of onlookers were such notables as Dave Morgan of TRAINS Magazine, both of the Claytor boys (Graham and Robert) plus many others.

Within 30 minutes the shiny ex-N&W Northern will be on home rails where, from 1950 to 1959, it pulled such famous trains as the *Powhatan Arrow, Pocahontas, Cavalier* and other varnish.

It would be the center of attention when it entered the "Citadel of Steam" for so many years after most railroads had dieselized: Roanoke!

The Roanoke Shops built 14 of the J's between 1941 and 1950 (the year of No. 611's birth). They were huge engines. In fact, the streamlined 600's turned out to be the most powerful non-articulate steam locomotives ever built. They boasted 80,000 lbs. of tractive effort, carried 300 lbs. of steam pressure and had 70" drivers which had been counterbalanced for speeds beyond 100 m.p.h. Standing nearly 16 feet tall and 110 feet long, No. 611's engine weight was approximately 494,000 pounds with its hefty tender, which carried 35 tons of coal and 20,000 gallons of water, being almost 378,600 lbs. For excursion work, No. 611 was assigned an extra tender (called a "canteen") which made an additional 20,800 gallons of the precious liquid available.

No. 611 was removed from regular service by the N&W in 1959 and placed on display in Roanoke in 1963. Then, in 1982, fire returned to its innards and it would resume service for excursion work until 1994 when the NS discontinued the popular program which was started by the Southern.

After all the "elbow grease" and "TLC," No. 611 looked as beautiful as the day it rolled out of the paint shop in Roanoke during the summer of 1950.

It was truly a "star" when it arrived in Roanoke later this same day. Actually, it was the "star" all the way from Birmingham and reigned as "The Queen" until 1994. She's now back at the Transportation Museum in Roanoke on display. This particular day in August of 1982, however, she was alive and making long lasting memories for thousands of railfans.

Curt Tillotson, Jr.

Hammering west towards Lynchburg, Va. after a stop at Crewe, Va., Extra 611 West is shown passing through Burkeville, Va. on the ex-Norfolk and Western's (now Norfolk Southern Corp.) Norfolk-Cincinnati mainline with 18 cars on May 18, 1985, at 11:35 a.m. with the temperature at a comfortable 74° F.

No. 611 was one of 14 ultra-modern and gracefully streamlined N&W J-class 4-8-4's built at the company's Roanoke Shops. The 4-8-4's were also equipped with roller bearings as well.

The 611 was the "Queen of the Excursions" from 1982 until the end of this popular 28 year program in 1994.

On this particular day, the bullet nose, steamboat whistle equipped 4-8-4 was on a Norfolk-Lynchburg-Altavista-Norfolk run carrying over 500 railfans on an occasion they will long remember.

The ground trembled beneath my feet as the "J" went by me at approximately 35-40 m.p.h. in a most dramatic fashion that even marveled and impressed this Southern Ps-4 class 4-6-2 fan. This was truly a photo that demonstrated the mystique of steam and steel in action. Wouldn't you agree?

Both: Curt Tillotson, Jr.

Extra 611 North-August 22, 1982-84° F—7 cars-12:05 p.m.— "Maiden Run" from Birmingham, Alabama to Roanoke, Va. to begin excursion work-shown leaving the ex-Southern Railway System's Washington-Atlanta mainline-just south of Lynchburg, Virginia's Mont-view Yard-and heading, on the connection track, to the ex-Norfolk and Western's Kinney Yard where it would eventually head west, on the last leg of its journey to the place of its birth: Roanoke, over the rails of the newly created Norfolk Southern Corp.

Articulation: "a joint or place between two parts where separation may take place spontaneously..." Such is the definition of this term in the *Random House College Dictionary*. In order for a long locomotive to negotiate a curve in the tracks, the engine must be able to articulate its long frame to successfully pass by the curve. This ability is clearly demonstrated in this photo.

Shown here is ex-Norfolk and Western class "A" 2-6-6-4 No. 1218, with its numerous consorts standing nearby, admiring this 1943 product of the Roanoke shops. The huge and long-approximately 122 feet without the "canteen" (extra tender)—"pride of the N&W" rests at Petersburg, Va.—at the site of the old passenger station-after completing the first half of its Norfolk, Va. to Petersburg roundtrip excursion on May 2, 1987, at 12:45 p.m. with 14 cars. In the photo, No. 1218 exhibited its ability to articulate the curve shown. This was an essential requirement when working through the mountains of Virginia and West Virginia. As a point of interest, most trains, especially the coal runs, by-passed the town to the south of Petersburg.

The "A's" were considered the "creme dé la creme" of the Norfolk and Western, hauling coal, merchandise and, when needed, passenger trains as well. With roller bearings on wheels, 300 lbs. of steam pressure, 114,000 lbs. of tractive effort and 70" drivers, these best of the 2-6-6-4 wheel arrangement, could do it all in a most efficient manner.

In 1986, the Norfolk Southern Corp. decided to reactivate No. 1218, which had been in retirement since 1959, and put it into excursion work since its J-class 4-8-4 No. 611 had proved so successful in this service. In April of 1987, it was introduced to the public and it proved to be a favorite among the fans.

On this particular day in 1987, No. 1218 had plenty of company with almost 400 passengers plus car loads of fans ready to follow and photograph the 2-6-6-4 on its trip back to Norfolk.

The Southern and Norfolk Southern fielded 2-8-0's, 2-8-2's, 4-6-2's, 4-6-4's, 2-8-4's, 2-10-4's, 4-8-4's and, on this day, a 2-6-6-4 in its steam excursion program. Other than the big Texan 2-10-4 (No. 610), No. 1218 presented a sight to behold! A real articulated steam engine-alive-and in action in the 1980's and 1990's! Remarkable! Thank you Southern and Norfolk Southern for a look back to a time when steam ruled the rails.

Curt Tillotson, Jr.

SOUTHERN RAILWAY

IN COLOR

On this particular day in March of 1952, Dave Driscoll grabbed his usual camera with the black and white film, plus the camera he used to make color slides and headed to the Reidsville station. Why two cameras? Dave had learned that local passenger train No. 11, had a PS-4 class 4-6-2 for its motive power. Our photographer knew that diesels were near to removing all steam power on the Southern, especially on its busy Washington-Atlanta mainline. So he felt he must take this opportunity to preserve on film these green and gold colored beauties one more time before they would be gone forever.

Dave's information was correct for he found the Richmond built (1926) No. 6482 at the head of the local and the "boys" at Monroe had cleaned her up. Indeed, the pleasing colors and white trim made one forget that this was old No. 11, not the *Crescent*, *Piedmont Limited* and the other members of the passenger fleet, and it was 1952, not the 1930s when the PS-4's were the common motive power used to move the Southern's renown varnish with style, dignity and speed.

Thank goodness this slide was made, for No. 6482 will be on the scrap track by August of 1953

Dave Driscoll/Author's Collection

Reidsville, N.C. could be described as a typical Southern town; however, two factors sets Reidsville apart from other similar communities: it was located on the Southern Railway's hot Washington-Atlanta mainline (24 miles south of Danville, Va. and 24 miles north of Greensboro, N.C.) and hosted a tremendous volume of trains, day and night, passenger and freights. The other factor was that it was the home of David Driscoll—rail photographer, rail historian "extraordinaire."

Dave took thousands of photos of the ebb and flow of rail traffic passing through his hometown during the days when steam ruled the rails. He even made numerous color slides of the action when the green and gold Ps-4 was queen of the Southern's passenger fleet and the big Ms-4, 2-8-2's were the main power for the vast majority of the freights that rumbled through the area. Rumble indeed, for there was a slight grade entering the town from the north and a stiff climb entering the town from the south. The people in Reidsville could hear the "stack talk" of the steamers and the "growl" of the diesels several minutes before the train passed through this location. Even today, Norfolk Southern's GM and GE's still make their appearance with great noise and fanfare.

Because of his efforts to record these moments in rail history, several of Dave's works appear in this book. He caught the green and gold beauties on film and the other motive power that made the Southern unique among all roads— north, south, east and west. Thanks Dave.

Shown here is No. 4811, a Ms-4 Mikado, leaving Reidsville and heading south to Greensboro's Pomona Yard as its fireman, seen standing on the tender, pushes coal toward the stoker screw. The Richmond build (1923) has charge of local No. 73 on October 4, 1951.

By '51, the diesels had command of almost 95% of all traffic on the mainline. Still the locals—freight and passenger—still had steam motive power. The big "Mike" will scrapped in April of 1952, so time grows short for the old girl. On this day, however, she still looked and sounded like a mainliner, in her prime.

Both: Dave Driscoll/Author's Collection

RIGHT:

Here she is "Queen" of the Pacifics" Southern Railway System's renown Ps-4 Class 4-6-2.

The date is May 12, 1950—very late in the steam era, especially on the Southern, since it was all-diesel by 1953.

Even at this late date, however, No. 6689 still had that eye-catching green and gold color scheme. Just look at those silver cylinder head! True, the Richmond built (1926) 4-6-2 was pulling the lowest of low runs, the stop at all stations, pickup everything No. 11, she was still beautiful even without the graphite on its smokebox.

Soon, that steamboat whistle will give two blasts and the former Alabama Great Southern assigned Ps-4—now in pool service—will depart Reidsville, N.C., head south and stop at the next station.

Although the diesels have bumped these ladies from the plush assignments, on this particular day we have the privilege of seeing one of the most beautiful locomotives ever built in action, in all its glory. Yes, although she was scrapped in December of 1950, No. 6689 was alive and well, on the mainline, doing what it did for 24 years. It was truly a great day for those who admired these "Queens."

LOCOMOTIVE WHEEL ARRANGEMENTS

Locomotives in the United States were identified by the Whyte System. For example, an engine whose wheels were arranged in a "oOOOOo" fashion meant two wheels were under the cylinders, eight driving wheels and two under the firebox; it was classified as a "2-8-2" and called a "Mikado."

The following is a listing of wheel arrangements found in this book:

0-6-0	=	Six wheel switcher
0-8-0	=	Eight wheel switcher
2-8-0	=	Consolidation
2-8-2	=	Mikado
2-8-4	=	Berkshire
2-10-2	=	Santa Fe
2-10-4	=	Texas
4-6-2	=	Pacific
4-6-4	=	Hudson
4-8-2	=	Mountain
4-8-4	=	Northern
2-6-6-6	=	Allegheny
2-6-6-4	=	Mallet
2-8-8-2	=	Mallet

Some railroads gave different names to their locomotive wheel arrangements. For example, the Chesapeake & Ohio called their 2-8-4's, "Kanawhas" and their 4-8-4's, "Greenbriers" while the Richmond, Fredericksburg & Potomac referred to their 4-8-4's as either "Governors" or "Generals" (depending on their size, weight, tractive effort, etc.). During World War II, some roads called their 2-8-2's "MacArthurs" rather than the more accepted "Mikado" tag. However, the Whyte System was the accepted classification given to the steam locomotive wheel arrangements by the vast number of railroads.

TOP LEFT:

Depicted in this photo is a railfan's heaven: dirt, grease, the wet smell of steam, partly cloudy on a mostly sunny day due to the smoke of so many locomotives, noise, the ground covered with cinders and unknown material, sand, etc. — BEAUTIFUL!

Amid all this debris we find a jewel: a green and gold colored, white trimmed Southern Railway System majestic Ps-4 class Pacific, No. 1395 (built by Richmond in 1926 and nearly 92 feet long from cowcatcher to tender coupler.)

The main passenger power for over two decades, No. 1395—shown riding the turntable at the Spencer, N. C. roundhouse on June 8, 1947—and her sisters are slowly being replaced (at an alarming pace) by the diesels—the motive power selected by the Southern to carry the road into the future.

It's a sure bet that No. 1395 is being prepared for a run to either Greenville, S.C. and Atlanta, Ga. or north to Lynchburg, Va and Washington since th line to Asheville, N.C. was dominated by 4-8-2's for passenger work and 2-10-2's for the freights.

How would it be to wander among such surroundings as show here once more? Wonderful!

Both: Dave Driscoll/Collection of T.W. Dixon, Jr.

BOTTOM LEFT:

The "ready track" area at Spencer, N.C. was **always** busy during the days of steam. After all, this railroad town was located about midway on the hot Southern Railway Washington-Atlanta mainline plus it had to provide power for the run to Asheville, N.C. and the "Land of the Sky."

Shown here on June 8, 1947, is a pair of Ms-4 class 2-8-2's after being inspected, coaled, watered, washed and made ready for another assignment. No. 4856, a Schenectady built (1924) Mikado, is ready to use its 326,000 lbs. of weight and 59,600 lbs of tractive effort to move more freight for the Southern. It could be a trip to Greenville, S.C. on the Charlotte Division or to Monroe, Va. or even to Selma, N.C. by way of Greensboro and Raleigh, N.C.—both on the Danville Division.

Look how clean the boys at Spencer had made her. The Ms-4's were the main freight power on the Southern for over 25 years. Only the diesels "put them out to pasture." Indeed, No. 4856 was scrapped in November of 1952, so this handsome 2-8-2 had only five years remaining to move the tonnage and put revenue into the coffers of the road that cared for them until the abilities of the diesel were proved. Once this was established, the days of steam were numbered.

Next to the Ps-4, the reliable Ms-4's were among the most admired of Southern's motive power. I agree 100% with this observation.

ABOVE:

To think that one could find such a clean, handsome looking 2-8-0 on the Southern Railway System by August 3, 1952, is truly hard to believe, since less than a year after this photo was made—at Greensboro, N.C.'s Pomona Yard—the road would be 100% dieselized.

By this time practically all trains were powered by the diesel. Only a few work trains and/or local freights plus, on those rare occasions when a diesel was not available, a local passenger run, was assigned to a steam locomotive. Such an situation usually resulted in a Ps-4 class 4-6-2 or Ms-4 2-8-2 being used, certainly not a lowly Consolidation. Yet, there she stood. No. 813 ready to go to work one more time.

The compact and efficient Ks-2 class 2-8-0 appears in near mint condition, even at this late date. The white trim, yellow numbering and lettering had the little 2-8-0 looking far better than when it arrived from Baldwin in 1910. Look at that enlarged tender, loaded "to the gills" with the stuff that made it run on the Southern for 43 years (she was scrapped in August, 1953—one year after this photo was made).

How refreshing it was to find such an attractive consolidation so very late in the life of steam power on the Southern.

RAILROAD COMMUNICATIONS

Before the advent of radios, train crews usually had basically two ways in communicating with one another: hand signals or through a whistle code.

The following whistle signals were among the most common used during the pre-radio days. In some cases, these signals can still be heard to this very day ("O" stands for short signal blast and "—" for a long):

0	=	Apply brakes. Stop-
— —	=	Release brakes. Proceed-
— 000	=	Flagman protect rear of train-
— — — —	=	Flagman may return from west or south-
— — — — —	=	Flagman may return from east or north-
00	=	Answer to any signal not otherwise provided for-
000	=	When standing, back; when running, stop at next station-
— — 0 —	=	Approaching public crossing at grade. To be prolonged or repeated until crossing is reached-
——	=	(Very long) - Approaching station, junction, railroad crossing, at grade and where otherwise required-
— — 0	=	Approaching meeting or waiting points (to be sounded one mile before meeting or waiting point)-
0 —	=	Inspect train line for leak or for brakes sticking-
000000	=	Alarm for persons or livestock on track (this is a succession of short blasts, no given number of signals)

There were other whistle signals prescribed in Rule 14 of the Association of American Railroads Standard Code; however, the ones included above were among the most often used.

Not only were the whistle codes implemented to "talk" to the crew, they were essential when a "helper" engine tied onto the rear of a train to help push it up and over a grade or on a double-header. The two (or more) engineers "talked" to each other by these whistle signals.

A train in a hurry! Southern's Ms-4 class 2-8-2, No. 4811, is leaving Reidsville, N.C. with great gusto and as fast as its 63" drivers could move. It looked like just another Washington-Atlanta mainline freight being pulled by the big Mikado which was the main freight power used by the Southern for over 25 years. Actually, this is a local freight (No. 72) and the date is October 10, 1951. So this scene was not a typical occurrence. Instead, it was a rare sight to see a steamer in action on a railroad being glutted by diesel motive power. As a result, the photographer was most fortunate in finding the Richmond built (1923) "Mike" still in service, even heading a local freight this late date for steam (No. 4811 was scrapped in April of 1952).

Why so much speed? There were three diesel powered hotshot freights behind this hard working local, so the engineer would try to get his train to Dundee, Va and clear of the mainline without delaying the "parade" of through freights on his tail (by the way, he made it!).

One good thing came out of this situation, however. After stopping and starting all day—a practice local freights must endure—old No. 4811 was able to "stretch her legs" and show just what she could do when she got the green light. The crew also got a good breeze in the cab for some relief from the fire in that big boiler—also a good thing.

And to think, this used to be a common sight in Reidsville, seven days a week, 365 days a year.

David Driscoll/Author's Collection

Once a locomotive received extensive repairs, the shop crew would run it back and forward, fast and slow, time and time again on a track near the roundhouse—all in an attempt to allow the new parts to fall into place and to make sure additional repairs would not be required. In fact, on occasion they would place the engine on a local freight which stopped and started with great frequency, going fast, going slow and making sure it was ready for regular service.

The procedure is shown in this photo of Ps-2 Class 4-6-2, No. 1209, at Spencer, N.C. on June 8, 1947. The little Pacific, freshly painted in green and gold and trimmed in white, was being tested by the shop crew in a most dramatic fashion.

Even though the larger Ps-4's were called "Queen of the Pacifics," I would like to call this dainty 4-6-2 the "Little Princess"

She was built by Richmond and, in my opinion, looks far better in this photo than she did in 1904 when it was placed on the Southern's roster. No. 1209 would be scrapped in January, 1952.

Until the arrival of the heavy Ps-4's the "P" class Pacifics held down nearly all the passenger assignments and performed with great élan.

Among all the dirt and grime shown in this portrait, Ps-2 No. 1209 looked extra good and would serve the Southern well until removed from the property in early 1952.

Both: Dave Driscoll/T.W. Dixon, Jr. Collection

The engineer on local freight No. 73 looks back to make sure his train is intact and the brakeman is heading his way so that he could prepare his steed to depart Reidsville, N.C. on the afternoon of June 6, 1947.

Even with diesels arriving on Southern's property in large batches, there were still a few runs that you would find steam power in command by 1947, such assignments as local freights, work trains, branch lines and even mainline local passenger trains.

A case in point is this big, Richmond built (1923) Ms-4 class 2-8-2, which had prowled these rails for nearly 26 years, usually at the head of the hotshot freights, now relegated to local freight work.

No. 4815 will have its train in Greensboro, N.C. after dark—putting in over twelve hours of working the industries and dodging through freights and passenger runs. Unfortunately, the big 2-8-2 will be scrapped in August of 1953, so she still has six years to continue serving the road that "Serves the South"

The Ms-4 class Mikados were good engines; however, the diesels were better—better in working but not in looks (in my opinion), and the 2-8-2's served the Southern well for many years. What more could one ask from a machine which was more human-like than any other device built by man?

All: David Driscoll/Author's Collection

RIGHT:

David Driscoll (and you and I) got lucky once again when, on October 23, 1951, he found Ps-4, No. 6482 heading local passenger train No. 11 at Reidsville, N.C. After taking his black and white exposures, he made a few color slides of this Richmond built (1926) 4-6-2 (thank goodness).

Even without the graphite covered smokebox, old No. 6482 still looked good and her green and gold colors with white trim produced a fine portrait, especially this late in the steam era on the Southern —an era that ended in 1953.

By this time the renowned Ps-4's could only be found on local passenger trains since the diesels had command of the Southern's main passenger fleet. Indeed, by 1951, several of No. 6482's sisters had already been scrapped. No. 6482's existence will end in August of 1953; however, until that time the green and gold colored heavy Pacifics gave a great deal of dignity to such lowly locals as No. 11.

Everything seemed so right with the Ps-4's, both in appearance and performance. We are indebted to Dave Driscoll for recording this scene (in color) so that others can enjoy and imagine how it must have been when these ladies ruled the mainline varnish fleet on a regular basis.

ost photos of Southern Railway System's famous Ps-4 class 4-6-2's were made at station stops, on display and in black and white exposures. Few shots were made of these beautiful, green and gold Pacifics in action AND color.

We are lucky to have a color view of this "Queen of The Pacifics" in action. Although No. 1397 was pulling local passenger train No. 20—north of Reidsville, N. C. in May of 1950—it still looked as if it was ready to power the *Crescent* or the other historic varnish of the Southern.

The Richmond built (1926) Pacific was running out what time it had left since the diesels were pushing all steam—even these elegant ladies—to the scrap lines on a daily basis. In fact, No. 1397 will succumb to the scrapper's torch in February, 1952 (less than two years after the portrait was made on the Southern's Washington-Atlanta mainline).

Thank goodness one Ps-4 was saved—No. 1401—and can now be viewed at the Smithsonian Institution in Washington, D.C. No. 1401 will allow many generations to come to understand why these green and gold colored engines were held in such high esteem. Indeed No. 1401 will preserve it and it's sister's well deserved reputations as being one of the most revered locomotives ever built.

Among those who admired Southern Railway System's motive power, the favorite Ms-4 class 2-8-2's were those that had the Elecso feedwater heater placed in front of their smokestacks. This appliance gave them a bigger and more robust look; they simply made the heavy "Mikes" look so right! In fact, next to the legendary Ps-4 Pacifics, the Ms-4's were among the most beloved of all Southern's steam power.

A prime example to explain this loyalty is shown here as the Baldwin built (1928) 2-8-2 heads north, pulling local freight No. 72 in the Reidsville, N.C. area on May 7, 1952.

Like the Ps-4's, the shop and engine crews showered the remaining 4800's with great care and affection. No. 4898 looks almost as good in this 1952 photo as it did in the 1930s and '40s when it was the main power for all of Southern's hottest freights.

While pulling this local freight on the Washington-Atlanta mainline, No. 4898 appears ready to power freights forever; even though at this late date for steam, diesels were rapidly replacing its sisters at an alarming pace. Just look at that white-trimmed pony truck!

All: David Driscoll/Author's Collection

The date: March 27, 1952; the location: Reidsville, N.C. (on the Southern Railway System's double track, Washington-Atlanta mainline-Danville Division); the train local passenger No. 11; the motive power: Steam-STEAM? Steam on the Southern in 1952? YES! Not only is it steam; it is a legendary Ps-4 Class 4-6-2, No. 1378 on the point.

With complete dieselization only a year away, on occasion the lowly local passenger train still rated a steam locomotive rather than one of the Southern's expensive diesels.

Looking at No. 1378, who would have thought that this green and gold colored beauty rolled out of the erecting shop at Schenectady in 1923? She still appears to be in her prime, even after running up and down the mainline for nearly 29 years. Unfortunately the heavy Pacific would be scrapped on October 17, 1952, not because she could not perform but because the diesel was here to stay—it was destined to be the future motive power for the Southern.

Even though the Elesco feedwater heater equipped Ps-4's were the most popular among the railfans, old No. 1378 with the big Worthington feedwater heater—seen above the third driver, still looks very attractive and will never be forgotten.

Almost all major roundhouses on the Southern Railway System had a "shop goat" during the age of steam operation. These little engines were converted from a regular switcher by removing its tender, putting water jackets on its sides and building a short extension on the rear to hold a small amount of coal—making them a "tank" engine.

Shown here is an 0-6-0T ('T': for tank) at the Spencer N.C. roundhouse area on June 8, 1947. This little "goat" was known as a A-1 class engine with 51" drivers and produced 15,915 lbs. of tractive effort. Built as a regular switcher by Pittsburgh in 1906, it was scrapped in November, 1949.

The "T's" rarely strayed from the roundhouse vicinity and were usually used to: push a road engine into a stall at the roundhouse for inspection and repairs if needed, then the "goat" would move the bigger engine to the coal and water facilities, push them through the wash track and finally place them on the ready track to wait for their next assignment.

The shop crews would lavish these "mighty mites" with as much attention as they did for the Ps-4's and Ms-4's. Indeed, look at the green and gold colored No. 1575 with white trim wheels. She was beautiful and served the Southern well until the diesel made it obsolete. It was a fine albeit unusual shaped locomotives.

Another rare action shot of a Southern Railway System's Ps-4: No. 1391 is shown departing Reidsville, N.C. with great gusto on September 8, 1951.

No. 1391 was built at Schenectady in 1924, and had local passenger train No. 11 well in hand this sunny morning in '51—late in the steam era which came to a sad conclusion in 1953. No. 1391 was finally scrapped during November, 1952—just slightly over a year after this dramatic portrait was preserved on film.

During the last few years before the diesel decimated Southern steam, the few remaining Ps-4's were usually found on local passenger trains, if diesels were not available. Such was the case of No. 11, the lowest of the low passenger assignments.

Here we have an engine which was among the major motive power for Southern's historic passenger fleet since the 1920s on a plug run. However, the green and gold colored 4-6-2 did not seem to be embarrassed by such a demotion. Instead, if you did not know the date of this photo, you would think the Ps-4s were still the No. 1 motive power for the Southern varnish.

I bet that everyone in Reidsville knew that No. 11 was leaving town since that stack talk was getting louder and producing a stirring staccato rhythm. This action probably caused the casual observer to stop whatever they were doing in order to watch this event which would disappear from the rails sooner than they could imagine.

This was a good day to be in Reidsville, that's for sure!

David Driscoll/Author's Collection

In Color

During the late 1950s, the Norfolk and Western officials made a major decision and it involved that six letter word: diesel!

Even though their fleet of steam locomotives, from their Class J 4-8-4's to the Class S1a 0-8-0's, were still operating in a most efficient manner, it was becoming more difficult to purchase and/or make parts to maintain their fleet of steamers. So the only option appeared to be the diesel. Indeed, the N&W placed one of the largest single orders ever received by GM for hundreds of GP-9's.

The road did not wait until all the road switchers arrived, they borrowed a large batch of "Geeps" from the Pennsylvania. They even, suddenly, replaced the Class J 4-8-4's with "E" units from both the ACL and RF&P in the summer of 1958.

Within a few months after these actions, the only steam remaining on the property were a few articulateds up in the coal country and even these powerful 2-8-8-2's were gone by mid-1960. In fact, only one "J" was preserved: No. 611 (built at Roanoke in 1950—only nine years old.)

The last N&W steam run I witnessed occurred in August, 1959 when the Appalachian Power Company rented the 611 to carry their families and several V.I.P.'s on a Roanoke-Norfolk round trip.

I caught the special taking on water at Crewe on it's return trip to Roanoke. Then my last shot was at the west end of Crewe yard and the 611 really put on a show. Indeed she was the last J in operating condition at the time.

Little did I know that in 1982, No.611 would join the excursion program of the Norfolk Southern Corporation and would remain in excursion service until the end of 1994. Today, this beautiful streamlined giant can be seen at the Virginia Museum of Transportation in Roanoke.

This last photo was an ideal way to end a great era of steam operations on the N&W. As Jackie Gleason might have said: "How Sweet it Was!"

Curt Tillotson, Jr.

Rushing east with a loaded coal train in the Roanoke Valley, Y6b No. 2188 is already an endangered species, the black invaders from LaGrange and Schenectady are already on the property in this late summer 1956 scene. Nothing appears to have changed from just a few years ago, but the onslaught has begun, and modern steam power such as this (built 1951) would be rapidly replaced by diesels in just a few short years. However, all is right within this railroad world and 2188 is doing just what she was designed for, hauling tonnage at a reasonable track speed.

T.W. Dixon, Jr. Collection

While the famous Norfolk and Western Class J's got the glory as N&W's passenger power, the near look-alike Class K2 was almost relegated to the background. After World War II, the railroad thought enough of these locomotives to invest heavily in modernizing and upgrading them. While the image of the *Powhatan Arrow* behind a Class J is the main thought when N&W passenger service is discussed, that seldom, if ever, produced revenue to the likes of the secondary trains. There are at least five cars of mail and express on the head end on this cloudy day. In just a few more years, K2a No. 136 will be replaced, not by diesels, at least at first, but by a Class J, which had been bumped from the premier passenger assignments in the summer of 1958.

Both: T.W. Dixon, Jr. Collection

A sight to behold! The ground is shaking as Y6b No. 2173 is heading up an eastbound drag crossing the Blue Ridge at the station named Blue Ridge, just east of Roanoke. N&W's usual practice was a Y class on the lead, a Class A, 2-6-6-4 following and another Y Class shoving hard behind the little red caboose at the rear of the train. The pusher (on the rear) would cut off on the fly, when the train has completely topped the summit and back to the "honey hole" to wait for the next eastbound train.

This was all part of the every day drama that occurred on the mountain in the days of steam. Today tonnage trains frequently travel eastbound on the former Virginian Railway which is built on a much easier gradient. Occasionally, when the former Virginian is closed off, modern diesels shake the ground here.

BIBLIOGRAPHY

Beebe, Lucius, *Highball*, New York: Bonanza Books, 1945.

Bryant, H. Stafford,Jr., *The Georgian Locomotive*, Barre, Massachusetts: Barre Gazette, 1962.

Dixon, Thomas W., Jr., *Chesapeake & Ohio Allegheny Subdivision*, Alderson, West Virginia: Chesapeake & Ohio Historical Society, Inc., 1985.

Gilbert, John F., *Crossties Over Saluda*, Raleigh, North Carolina: The Crossties Press, 1971.

Griffin, William E., Jr., *One Hundred Fifty Years of History Along the Richmond, Fredericksburg & Potomac*, Richmond, Virginia: Whittet & Shepperson, 1984.

Griffin, William E., Jr., *Richmond, Fredericksburg & Potomac*, Lynchburg, Virginia: TLC Publishing, Inc., 1994.

Huddleston, Eugene L. and Thomas W. Dixon, Jr., *The Allegheny-Lima's Finest*, Edmond, Washington: Hundman Publishing, 1984.

Huxtable, Nils and Thomas R. Schultz, *Steam Spirit*, A Steamscenes Publication, 1985.

Jeffries, Lewis Ingles, *Norfolk & Western: Giant of Steam*, Boulder, Colorado: Pruett Publishing Co., 1980.

Krause, John and H. Reid, *Rails Through Dixie*, San Marino, California: Golden West Books, 1965.

LeMassena, Robert A., *Articulated Steam Locomotives of North America*, Silverton, Colorado: Sundance Books, 1979.

Prince, Richard E., *Norfolk & Western-Pocahontas Coal Carrier*, Millard, Nebraska: Richard E. Prince, 1980.

Prince, Richard E., *The Richmond-Washington Line and Related Railroads*, Millard Nebraska: Richard E. Prince, 1973.

Prince, Richard E., *Seaboard Air Line Railway*, Green River, Wyoming: Richard E. Prince, 1969.

Prince, Richard E., *Southern Railway System Steam Locomotives and Boats*, Green River, Wyoming: Richard E. Prince, 1970.

Ranks, Harold E. and Shelby F. Lowe, *Southern Railway Steam Power*, Omaha, Nebraska: Barnhart Press, 1966.

Reid, H., *Extra South*, Morristown, New Jersey: Compton Press, 1964.

Reid, H., *The Virginian Railway*, Milwaukee, Wisconsin: Kalmbach Publishing Co., 1961.

Rosenberg, Ron and Eric H. Archer, *Norfolk & Western Steam (The Last 25 Years)*, New York City: Quadrant Press, 1972.

Shuster, Philip, Eugene L. Huddleston and Alvin Staufer, *Chesapeake & Ohio*, Carrolton, Ohio: Alvin Staufer, 1965.

TIES Magazine, Washington, D. C.: Southern Railway System, Vol. I-Vol. VII (1947-1953) and Vol. XVI, (1962).

TRAINS Magazine, Milwaukee and Waukesha, Wisconsin: Kalmbach Publishing Col, Vol. I thru Vol. LXI, 1940-1996.

Warden, William E., *Norfolk & Western A and J*, Andover, New Jersey: Andover Junction Publication, 1987.

Ziel, Ron and Mike Eagleson, *Southern Steam Specials*, Bloomfield, New Jersey: C. F. Wood Co., 1970.

The midday sun is beating down on this fine spring day as Y6 No. 2133 takes time freight 85 westbound near Elliston, Virginia. The location is actually closer to Kumis, located almost directly behind the locomotive, across the river, a location on the Virginian mainline. The stock cars at the head end are somewhat of a rarity on the N&W, often used for non-livestock products on the railroad, including brick and crossties.

T.W. Dixon, Jr. Collection

Right: The system map of the
Atlantic Coast Line from
1952.

K. L. Miller Collection

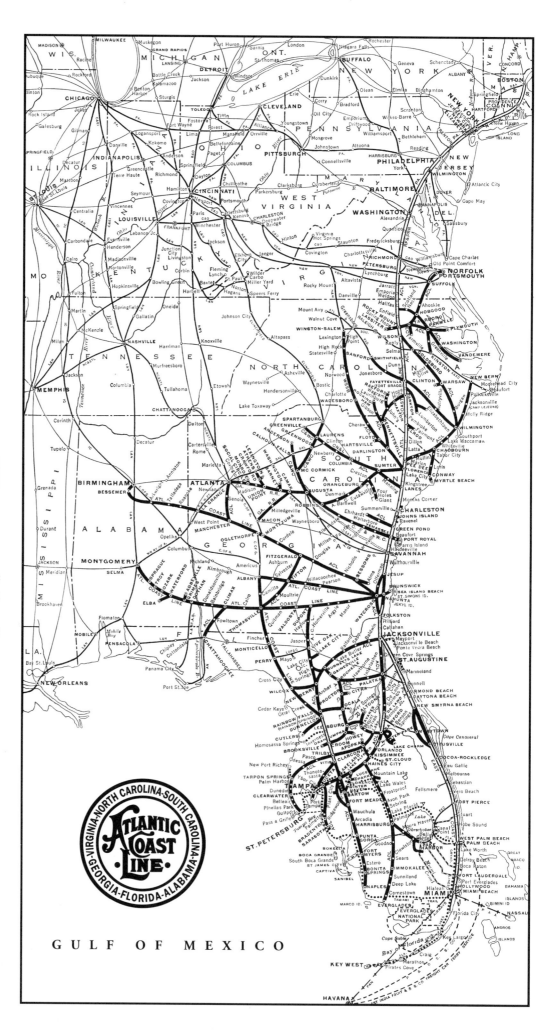